Collins

T0337207

SOCIAL STUDIES
Atlas
FOR THE CARIBBEAN

Workbook

Series editor: **Farah Christian**

Collins

William Collins' dream of knowledge for all began with the publication of his first book in 1819. A self-educated mill worker, he not only enriched millions of lives, but also founded a flourishing publishing house. Today, staying true to this spirit, Collins books are packed with inspiration, innovation and practical expertise. They place you at the centre of a world of possibility and give you exactly what you need to explore it.

Collins. Freedom to teach.

Published by Collins
An imprint of HarperCollins*Publishers*
Westerhill Road
Bishopbriggs
Glasgow G64 2QT

Browse the complete Collins Caribbean catalogue at
www.collins.co.uk/caribbeanschools

© HarperCollins*Publishers* Limited 2019

10 9 8 7 6 5 4 3 2 1

ISBN 978-0-00-836172-3

British Library Cataloguing in Publication Data
A catalogue record for this publication is available from the British Library.

The publishers gratefully acknowledge the permission granted to reproduce the copyright material in this book. Every effort has been made to trace copyright holders and to obtain their permission for the use of copyright material. The publishers will gladly receive any information enabling them to rectify any error or omission at the first opportunity.

Series editor: Farah Christian
Authors: Stephen Scoffham and Paula Owens
Publisher: Dr Elaine Higgleton
Project manager: Julianna Dunn
Copy editor: Mitch Fitton
Proofreader: Lucy Hyde
Typesetter: QBS Learning
Production controller: Alistair McKnight
Printed and bound by Grafica Veneta SpA

Contents

Introduction 4

Plan views 5
Different types of map 6
Map symbols 7
Features map 8
Different types of information 9
School information 10
Large and small scale maps 11
Using a scale bar 13
Different hemispheres 15
Longitude and latitude 16
Time zones 17
Grid references 18
Direction finder 19
Directions and distances 20
The seasons 21

The Caribbean political 22
The Caribbean physical 24
Hurricanes 26
Caribbean earthquakes 27
Volcano model – Photocopiable page 28
Caribbean energy and minerals 30
Caribbean population and languages 31
Caribbean tourism 32
Caribbean history and heritage 33
African enslavement in the Caribbean 34
Threats to the environment 37
Learning about the environment 38
The Bahamas 39
A cruise in the Bahamas 40
People in the Bahamas 41
Cuba – True of false? 42
Exploring the Cayman Islands 43
Jamaica features 44
Jamaica climate 45
Reviewing the history, culture
     and tourism of Jamaica 46
Haiti and Dominican Republic 47
Different histories 48
Puerto Rico 49
US Virgin Islands 50
Caribbean Island cube –
     Photocopiable page 51
Caribbean Islands word search 52
St Kitts cross section 53
Place names 54
Antigua 55
Antigua and Barbuda facts 56
Exploring Guadeloupe 57

Exploring Dominica 58
Mount Pelée 59
Settlements in St Lucia 60
Island chain 61
Spice Island 62
Barbados economic activity 63
All about Barbados 64
The ABC Islands 65
Trinidad and Tobago -True or false? 66
Trinidad and Tobago in numbers 67
Rain shadow 68
Trinidad mystery tour 69
Reviewing the history, tourism and
     culture of Trinidad 70
Guyana fact file 72
The River Essequibo 73
Guyana grid squares 74
Finding out about Belize –
     Photocopiable page 75
Central America in maps 76
Central America in words 77
North American cities 78
North America physical features 79
South American countries 80
South American capital cities 81
Africa map 82
Africa countries game –
     Photocopiable page 83
Europe grid squares 84
European journeys 85
Asian countries A-Z 86
Asia physical features 87
Oceania latitude and longitude 88
Coral Islands and Volcanic Islands 89
Antarctica 90
World countries 91
Country card game – Photocopiable page 93
Continents 94
Mountains 95
Four different climates 96
World winds 97
World vegetation 98
In the tropical forest 99
Moving plates 100
Hidden hazards 101
Serious issues 102
Picture tower – Photocopiable page 103
Cities worldwide 104
Mega cities 105
My Caribbean map 106
World map 107
Skills Index 108
Atlas Index 113

Introduction

This workbook is designed for use with Collins *Social Studies Atlas for the Caribbean* to help pupils learn about the geography and heritage of the Caribbean and the wider world. Activities are linked directly to a specific page in the atlas and introduce or consolidate different skills. The activities are aimed at pupils from upper primary to lower secondary age.

The workbook covers the five sections of the atlas: the opening section introduces atlas map skills; the next section focuses on the geography, history, and heritage of the Caribbean; locational maps and data about individual Caribbean islands form the central section of the workbook; and the last two sections consist of continental studies and a global overview. Environmental issues are woven into the activities as appropriate throughout the book.

The workbook provides support for different curriculum areas including English, social studies, geography, history and STEM/STEAM subjects. Teachers will be able to draw on the activities systematically and use them to enhance pupils' individual studies. The content is organised to correspond chronologically with the atlas, however teachers can also use the Skills Index at the back of this workbook if they would prefer to build their lessons by skill. This index is especially helpful for teacher and student alike when it comes to brushing up on specific skills that students need more practice in.

Each topic starts with a simple question that sets the scene and outlines its scope. Students can consider this question themselves if working alone, or the teacher can pose it to the class at the beginning of the lesson to engage students with the topic. The activities which follow enable the pupils to explore this question in different ways. Students are often directed to corresponding pages in their atlas for close reading of text and maps, and some activities involve map making and general cartographic skills. Work on symbols, compass directions, routes, grid squares, cross sections, and latitude and longitude is included where appropriate. Students are asked to draw graphs, process data, or extract information from the text in the atlas.

STEAM/STEM activities feature heavily throughout the workbook from Extended Learning exercises which build on research skills, to model-making using cut-outs from photocopiable pages. Games and quizzes have been included along with questions for discussion and issues for debate.

Plan views

What can you show on a plan of your classroom or playground?

1 **Look at the different plan views on page 2 of your atlas.**

Using this style of map, create a plan view of your own classroom or playground.

Think carefully about how you will use shape and colour to convey the type and relative size of features.

Are all maps the same?

1 **Working from page 3 of your atlas, complete the questions below.**

(a) Political maps show the size and location of _____.

(b) Physical or relief maps show _____, _____, rivers, lakes and the height of the _____.

(c) Graduated colour maps use colours to show a _____ or _____.

(d) Distribution maps show the distribution of _____ or _____ features.

(e) Satellite images show the Earth from 500 km above the surface.

What is the difference between a satellite image and a map?

_____

2 **Identify the type of map(s) shown on these pages of your atlas.**

ATLAS PAGE	MAP TYPE
58	
61	
41	
24	
49	
82–83	
14	
31	

Map symbols

What are the different symbols that are used on maps?

1 **(a)** Working from pages 4 and 5 of your atlas, draw symbols for the different features in the spaces below. Use appropriate colours for each symbol.

STANDARD FEATURES		SPECIAL FEATURES		INDUSTRY	
Capital city		National park		Cement works	
Important town		Point of interest		Chemicals	
Highway		Major resort		Oil refinery	
Airport		Port		Light industry	
Lake		Cruise ship		Oilfield	
Summit		Lighthouse		Gasfield	

(b) Name the parish in which the capital city of Trinidad, Port of Spain, is found. _____

(c) In the parish of Mayaro, what is the name of the important town found close Galeota Point. _____

(d) What is the name of the important town in which the international airport can be found? _____

2 **Now make up some map symbols of your own.**

Study area		Shops		Beach	
Play area		Park		Danger area	

What can you show on a features map of your area or country?

1 Use the atlas index to find a features map of your island or the place where you live.

(a) How many national parks are shown on the map of your island? _____

(b) Name FIVE places of interest.

_____

_____

2 Draw your own features map below.

Use symbols and add a key to explain what they mean.

Give your map a title.

3 Extended Learning

Conduct research on ONE place of interest and write a short report on the activities carried out there. Your report may include a description of its location and why it is considered a place of interest.

Different types of information

How does an atlas convey different types of information?

1. State how each of the different items in the table below conveys useful information.

ITEM	WHAT MAKES IT USEFUL?
Location maps	
Photographs	
Map keys	
Fact boxes	
Graphs and tables	
Text	

2. (a) Which THREE types of information might be particularly useful to a tourist?

_____

_____

_____

   (b) Explain why a tourist would find these types of information useful.

_____

_____

_____

3. (a) Which THREE types of information might be particularly useful to a politician?

_____

_____

_____

   (b) Why would these types of information be useful to a politician?

_____

_____

_____

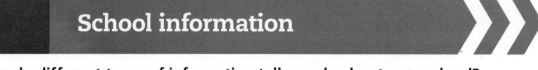

How do different types of information tell people about your school?

1 Draw a simple location map to show your school in relation to the area or country where you live.

2 Make up a simple fact box about your school. Note five (5) important facts about your school.

FACTS ABOUT MY SCHOOL

3 Draw a pie chart to show the proportion of girls and boys in your class.

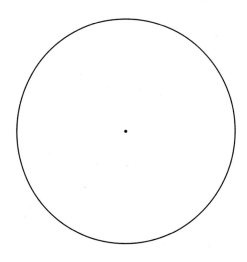

Large and small scale maps

What are the differences between large and small scale maps?

1 Identify the TWO ways in which the scale on a map may be shown.

_____

2 Complete these sentences.

(a) Large scale maps show a _____ _____ in detail.

(b) Small scale maps show a _____ _____ in much less detail.

3 Compare Maps A and B on page 6.

(a) Which of the two maps shows greater detail?

_____

(b) State some of the information shown by Map A that we would not get from Map B.

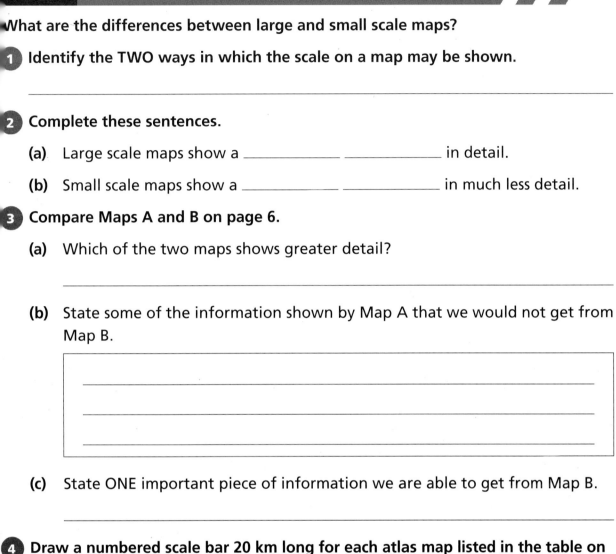

(c) State ONE important piece of information we are able to get from Map B.

_____

4 Draw a numbered scale bar 20 km long for each atlas map listed in the table on the next page. Write down the scale ratio underneath. You will need to do some calculations to understand how long your scale should be.

LARGE SCALE MAPS	
Grenada page 42	

Guadeloupe page 39	
St Lucia page 41	
SMALL SCALE MAPS	
Asia political page 66	
North America political page 58	
Europe political page 64	

Brain Teaser

Why do maps have different scales?

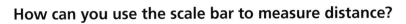

Using a scale bar

How can you use the scale bar to measure distance?

1 What is the distance between the following capital cities in the Caribbean (use pages 10–11 of your atlas)?

(a) I would have to travel _____ from St George's, Grenada for the annual Carnival in Port of Spain, Trinidad.

(b) To get to Castries in St Lucia from Kingston, Jamaica, the airline first travels to St John's, Antigua _____km away and then to Bridgetown, Barbados, which is _____km away. Travelling for _____km, another airline then takes us to Castries from Bridgetown.

(c) The Dominican Republic and Puerto Rico both are both Spanish speaking countries.

How far would Puerto Ricans in San Juan have to travel to attend a conference in Santo Domingo in the Dominican Republic?

_____

2 Use compass directions and the scale bar to help you find and name these places on the map of Trinidad on page 4 of your atlas.

(a) A mountain 940 metres high and 30 km west of Balandra Bay.

_____

(b) A body of water 20 km south of the answer to (a).

_____

(c) A city 30 km northwest of the answer to (b).

_____

(d) A range of hills around 75 km southeast of the answer to (c).

_____

(e) A bay 20 km north-east of the answer to (d).

_____

3 Draw symbols and labels on the outline map below to show the places and features given in the answers to question 2.

4 Complete your map by adding a key, compass and other major features.

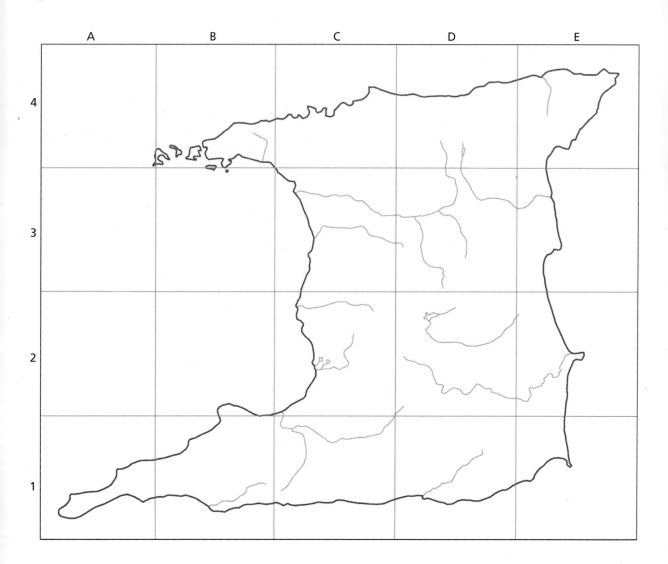

Different hemispheres

How is the world divided into hemispheres?

1 Find the Caribbean Islands (Cuba and Hispaniola) on the map below and colour them green. Which hemisphere are they in?

_____

2 Insert the Greenwich Meridian on the map below using a red line.

3 Using pages 74 and 75 of your atlas, label the TWO continents that are entirely in the Western Hemisphere. Colour them purple.

4 Now insert the Equator on the map below using a red line.

5 Which continent is almost equally divided between the Northern and Southern Hemispheres? Colour this continent orange and label it.

6 Which TWO continents lie entirely in the Southern Hemisphere? Colour them yellow and label them.

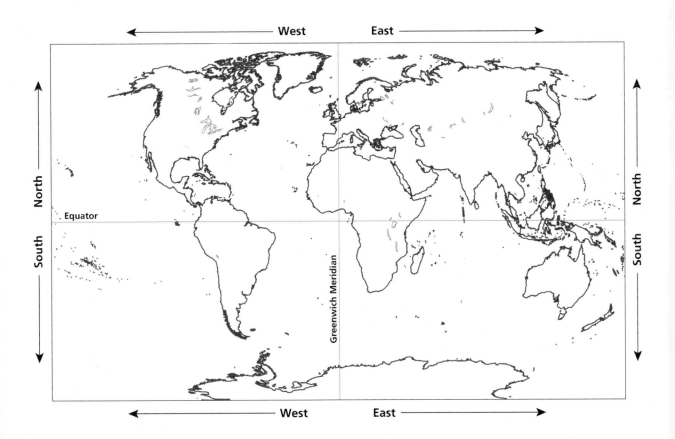

How are latitude and longitude used to locate places?

1 Using pages 72 and 73 of your atlas, find the latitude of these cities. Remember to say if each one is north (N) or south (S) of the Equator.

CITY	LATITUDE	CITY	LATITUDE
Beijing		Sucre	
St Petersburg		Anchorage	
Mexico City		Mauritius	
Wellington		Suva	
Nay Pyi Taw		Ankara	

2 Now find the longitude of these cities. Remember to say if each one is west (W) or east (E) of the Greenwich Meridian.

CITY	LONGITUDE	CITY	LONGITUDE
Seattle		Tokyo	
Port of Spain		Asmara	
Cape Town		Buenos Aires	
Manilla		Quito	
Panama City		Muscat	

3 Complete this table by naming the country you can find at these latitudes and longitudes.

LATITUDE AND LONGITUDE	COUNTRY	LATITUDE AND LONGITUDE	COUNTRY
40° N 100° W		20° N 100° W	
20° S 100° E		40° N 100° E	
60° N 100° E		0° 40° E	
20° N 80° E		40° N 0°	

4 Extended Learning

Lines of latitude and longitude help us to locate places exactly but they also help us to understand different things about the Earth. Conduct research to find out more about the following: Characteristics of lines of latitude and longitude. How lines of latitude help us to understand climate and the different climate zones.

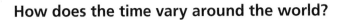
How does the time vary around the world?

1 Answer these questions, using page 7 in your atlas.

(a) Why does time vary around the world?

_____

(b) How many standard time zones are there? _____

(c) What is the time difference between each zone? _____

(d) What is the time at longitude 0° known as? _____

2 If it's 12 noon in London (Greenwich Mean Time), what time is it in other parts of the world?

Draw the correct times on the clocks.

Los Angeles   Sao Paolo   London   Jakarta   Sydney

am/pm   am/pm   pm   am/pm   am/pm

3 Complete this sentence using the following words:

noon	early morning	late evening	night-time

When it is 12 _____ in London, it is _____

in Sao Paulo, _____ in Beijing and _____

in Sydney.

4 If the time in the Caribbean now is _____ (check your current time), work out the time in:

Miami _____

London _____

Cape Town _____

Los Angeles _____

Singapore _____

Grid references

How do grid references help us find places?

Along with using latitude and longitude we sometimes use grid references to locate places in an atlas. Each grid is identified using a letter at the top and bottom of the map, and a number on either side of the map. To give the grid reference of a place we state the letter and then the number for the grid.

1 Using the Caribbean Political map on pages 10–11, work out the grid reference for the following places. (The first one is done for you.)

Georgetown, Guyana: H2   Belmopan, Belize: _____

Havana, Cuba: _____   Caracas, Venezuela: _____

Kingston, Jamaica: _____   Roseau, Dominica: _____

2 The grid reference for each place will change on different maps and can also be found in the atlas index. Use the atlas index to find the country, map page, and grid reference for the places in the table below.

PLACE	COUNTRY	MAP PAGE	GRID REFERENCE
San Juan			
Punta Gorda			
Castries			
Havana			
Quito			
Kiev			
Wellington			

3 Find and name the grid reference for these features on the physical map of the Caribbean on pages 12–13 in the atlas.

(a) The highest peak in the Caribbean Islands, Pico Duarte. _____

(b) The mouth of the longest river in the Caribbean Islands, River Cauto.

_____

(c) The island of Jamaica. _____

(d) The island of Barbados. _____

(e) Milwaukee Deep. _____

What lies in different compass directions?

1 Colour the direction finder below. Label the compass points E, S, W and NE, SE, SW and NW.

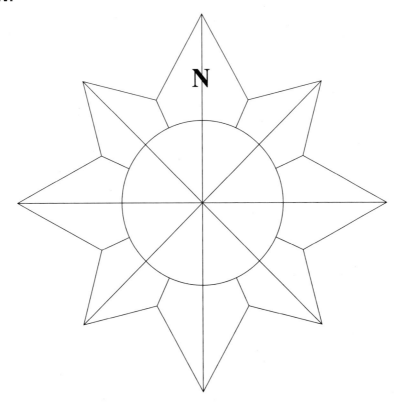

2 Use your direction finder to find out which countries and oceans lie in different compass directions from the given cities below. Make up a chart of your own.

COMPASS DIRECTION	GEORGETOWN Atlas page 60	WARSAW Atlas page 64
N		
NE		
E		
SE		
S		
SW		
W		
NW		

Directions and distances

What can you find in different compass directions?

1 **Using pages 58 and 59 of your atlas, work out the answer to these questions.**

What lies in different compass directions from Washington DC?

(a) 4000 km to the northwest: _____

(b) 2000 km to the south: _____

(c) 800 km to the southwest: _____

(d) 6500 km to the north: _____

(e) 2000 km to the northeast: _____

2 **Turn to pages 10 and 11 of your atlas.**

Find out what places and countries lie in these compass directions from Kingston, Jamaica.

(a) North of Kingston: _____

(b) South of Kingston: _____

(c) East of Kingston: _____

(d) West of Kingston: _____

3 **Look at a map of the area where you live. Name the places that are around you using different compass directions.**

In what part of the world is the Sun sometimes directly overhead?

1 Using pages 8–9 of your atlas, answer the questions below about the seasons.

(a) Explain what is meant by 'The Earth's axis is tilted from the perpendicular'.

_____

(b) What is the result of the Earth's axis being tilted?

_____

(c) Which of the seasons begins around June 21 and December 21 each year?

_____

(d) Outline THREE differences between what happens on June 21 and on December 21 each year.

_____

_____

_____

(e) What are TWO similarities between Autumn and Spring and what takes place on March 21 and September 21?

_____

_____

(f) Use the diagram of the seasons on page 9 to complete the table below.

DATE	SEASON IN NORTHERN HEMISPHERE	SEASON IN SOUTHERN HEMISPHERE	HOURS OF SUNLIGHT AT NORTH POLE	HOURS OF SUNLIGHT AT SOUTH POLE
March 21				
June 21				
September 21				
December 21				

2 Using pages 72 and 73 of your atlas, name some countries which lie within the Tropics where the Sun is sometimes directly overhead.

_____

_____

Which countries make up the Caribbean?

1 Write the names of the main countries and their capitals in the Greater Antilles in the chart below.

GREATER ANTILLES

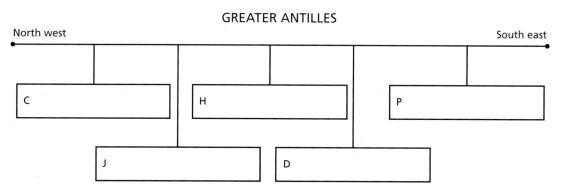

North west   South east

| C | | H | | P |

| J | | D |

2 Write the names of FIVE of the countries and their capitals in the Lesser Antilles in the next chart.

LESSER ANTILLES

North   South

| A | | St | | T |

| D | | G |

3 Record in the table when each country gained its independence.

COUNTRY	INDEPENDENCE DATE	COUNTRY	INDEPENDENCE DATE

Brain Teaser

What does it mean when a country is described as *independent*?

4 Name FOUR countries that have yet to gain their independence.

_____ , _____ , _____ , _____

5 Name the country that has been independent:

–   the longest   _____

–   the shortest   _____

6 On the map of the Caribbean below, complete the following.

–   Circle the countries of the Greater Antilles and label the grouping.

–   Circle the countries of the Lesser Antilles and label the grouping.

–   Circle and label the Bahamas and Turks and Caicos.

–   Shade all the independent territories blue.

–   Shade all the other territories yellow.

–   Label the Caribbean Sea and Atlantic Ocean.

–   Complete the map with a title, key and direction point.

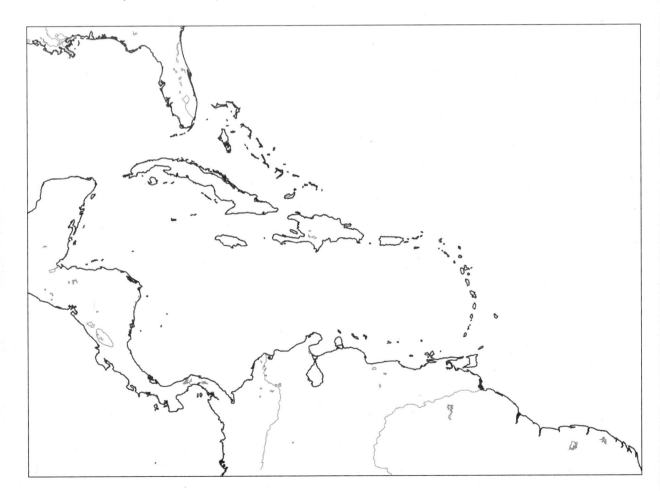

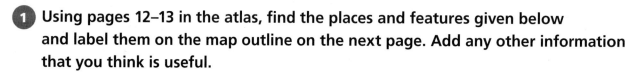

The Caribbean - physical

Which are the main islands in the Caribbean?

1. **Using pages 12–13 in the atlas, find the places and features given below and label them on the map outline on the next page. Add any other information that you think is useful.**

Caribbean Sea

Atlantic Ocean

Cuba

Hispaniola

Jamaica

Puerto Rico

The Bahamas

Trinidad

South America

Lesser Antilles

Leeward Islands

Windward Islands

Gulf of Mexico

Milwaukee Deep

Pico Duarte

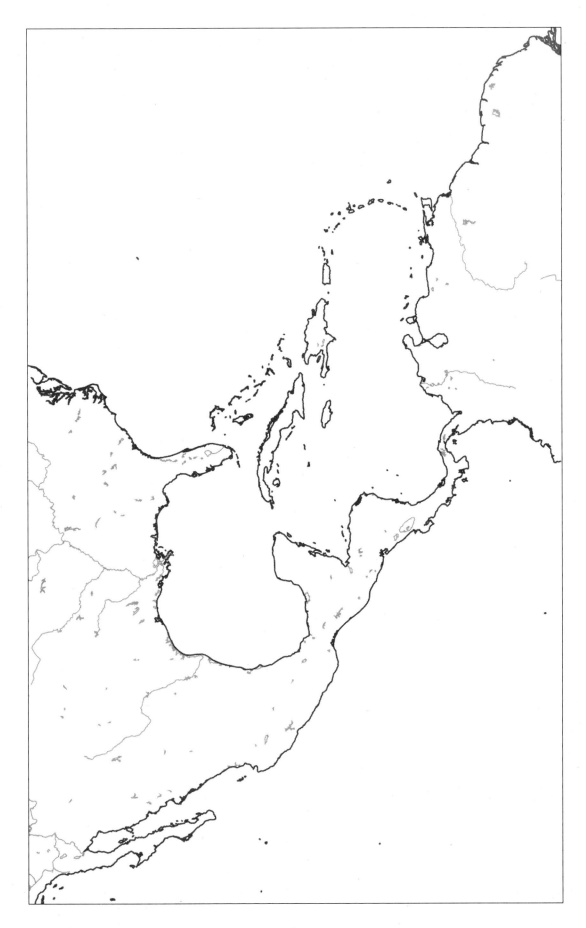

How is the Caribbean affected by hurricanes?

1 Look at the map of hurricane tracks on page 15 of your atlas.

(a) What do they have in common? _____

_____

(b) Some hurricanes may develop in the Caribbean Sea.

Name TWO such hurricanes and the year they occurred.

_____

(c) Which year had the most hurricanes? _____

(d) Which Caribbean island is least affected by hurricanes? _____

(e) Name the hurricanes that have affected your country. _____

2 Find Hurricane Matthew on the map on page 15 in the atlas. Copy its track onto the map here.

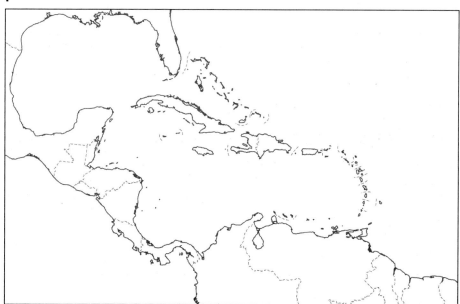

3 Write a news headline about Hurricane Matthew and the damage it caused.

Use the text, facts and diagrams on page 15 to help you.

Why do the Caribbean islands suffer from earthquakes?

1 **Complete these sentences**

(a) The world's _____ occur most frequently at plate boundaries.

(b) The Caribbean islands are located on the _____ of the Caribbean plate.

(c) When the Caribbean plate _____ relative to its neighbours, it causes an _____.

2 **Working from page 16 of your atlas, label and colour the earthquake diagram below.**

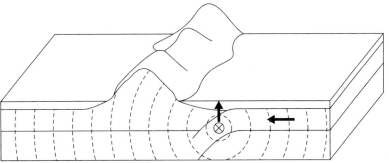

3 **Discuss how the place where you live is affected by earthquakes.**

4 **Annotate this map of the Caribbean to capture the location, magnitude and number of deaths for these earthquakes:**

- Kingston – 1907

- Trinidad – 1997

- Haiti – 2010.

5 **Extended Learning**

Use the internet to find out more about the following features of an earthquake:

focus / focal point
epicentre
shockwaves

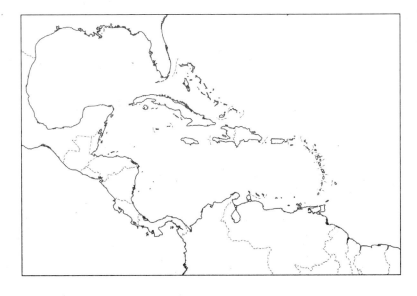

What is the structure of a typical volcano?

1 **Colour a photocopy of the cut-out volcano model below.**

Use different colours for the layers of lava and ash and for the trees and rocks along the slopes.

2 **Cut out the photocopied model carefully and fold along the dotted lines.**

3 **Complete the model by gluing the flap underneath the opposite side.**

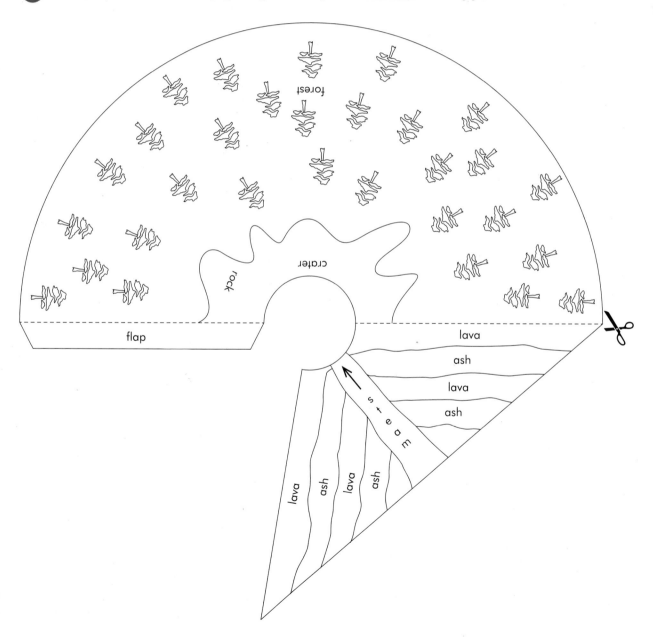

4 Name TWO non-volcanic islands in the Lesser Antilles.

_____

_____

5 Which tiny island has more than four volcanoes?

_____

6 Name the island that has had the most recent eruption and state the year of the eruption.

_____

7 Annotate the map of the Caribbean below to capture the current status, last eruption, number of deaths or amount of damage from last eruption of the volcanoes in Montserrat and Martinique.

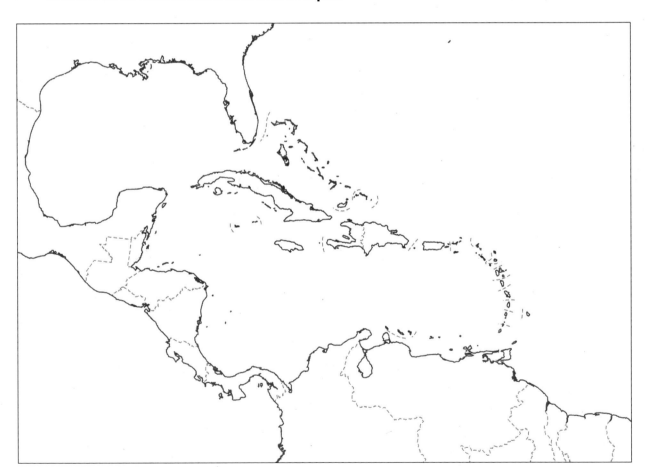

Caribbean energy and minerals

What are the energy and mineral resources in the Caribbean?

1 Using page 18 of your atlas, compete the energy and minerals table below.

Look at each country in turn and tick below each resource that it has.

COUNTRY	OIL	GAS	BAUXITE	GOLD/ SILVER	NICKEL
TOTAL					

2 Working from the table and the map on page 18, which resources are most abundant?

_____

3 Working from the number of symbols on the map, which countries have the most energy and mineral resources?

_____

What are the main languages spoken in the Caribbean?

1 Complete the table below by writing down the population of each country in the table to the nearest million and the main language for each

COUNTRY	POPULATION (million)	MAIN LANGUAGE
Cuba		
Haiti		
Dominican Republic		
Puerto Rico		
Jamaica		
Trinidad and Tobago		
Guyana		
Suriname		

2 Draw a bar graph to show the population of each country. Label each column.

3 Colour the graph and the key below.

Key	
Spanish	☐
French	☐
English	☐
Dutch	☐

4 Using the population information in the table above, which language is spoken by most people?

_____

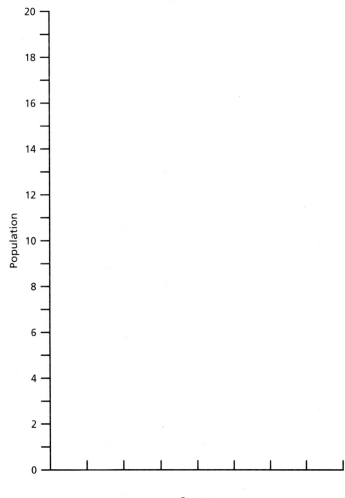

What routes do cruise ships follow?

1 Draw these cruise ship routes on the map below using different colours:

    (a)   the route from Fort Lauderdale

    (b)   the route from Barbados.

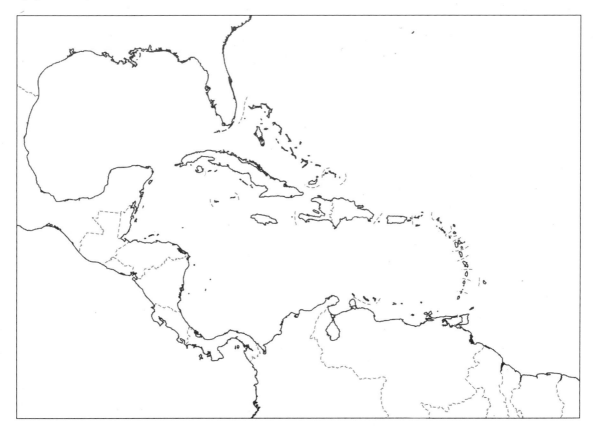

2 Label the stops on each route.

3 Make up your own cruise ship route.

    Use another colour to show it on the map. Label the stops.

4 Name the countries that are major cruise ship destinations.

_____

5 Which country had the highest number of stopover visitors and cruise ship stops in 2014?

    Stopover: _____

    Cruise ship stops: _____

Caribbean history and heritage

What do you know about the original inhabitants of the Caribbean? Use pages 20–21 of your atlas.

1 **On this map of the Caribbean:**

(a) Label the areas where the Aztec, Inca and Maya lived in Central and South America.

(b) Shade the areas occupied by the Tainos in yellow and those occupied by the Caribs in blue.

(c) Insert arrows to show the movement of the Amerindians into the Caribbean from South America.

(d) Give your map an appropriate title and key.

2 **Extended Learning**

Use the internet and other resources to find out the following:

– Which Amerindian group settled where you live?

– How did these people live (economic activities, government and social life)?

When did different events happen in our history?

3 **Sequencing: Using the numbers 1 to 5, place these events in the order in which they occurred:**

Christopher Columbus first landed in the Bahamas. ◯

Migration of people from Asia to America across the Bering Strait. ◯

Viking village of L'Anse aux Meadows in Newfoundland established. ◯

4.5 million Africans were forced to settle in the Caribbean. ◯

Carib and Taino people migrated northwards from South America to Jamaica, Cuba and the Bahamas. ◯

4 **Extended Learning**

Visit your school or local library or browse the internet. In your journal, write a brief description of who the Vikings were and four points that suggest the Viking village of L'Anse aux Meadows existed.

What is the history of African enslavement in the Caribbean?

1 How long was the period of enslavement for Africans who were brought to the Americas? Calculate the answer in number of years. _____

2 What is the approximate number of Africans who were captured from West Africa? _____

3 How many enslaved Africans ended up in the Caribbean? _____

4 The journey across the Atlantic for the enslaved Africans lasted for three months.

Write TWO paragraphs to capture what you think the journey was like and the difficulties they faced.

_____

_____

_____

_____

_____

_____

Why is the Caribbean so diverse?

> **Brain Teaser**
> **Do you know what is meant by cultural diversity?**

5 **(a)** Complete the map on the next page to show the different groups of people that migrated to the Caribbean.

   – Label the different continents

   – Label the following countries: Britain (now United Kingdom), Spain, France, Portugal, India, China, Syria, Sierra Leone, Nigeria, Ghana, Indonesia

   – Insert arrows to show the route taken by different groups into the Caribbean

   – Shade the countries from which the largest group of people came freely

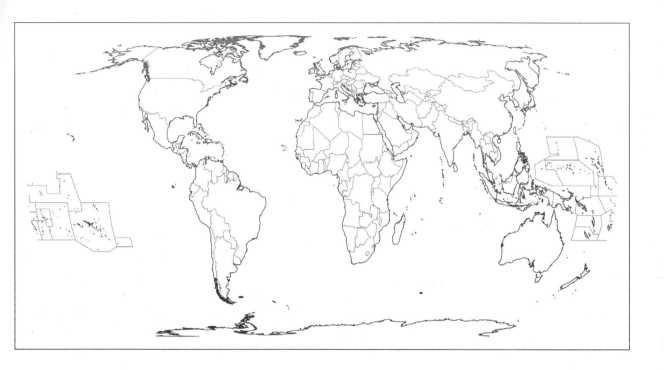

(b) Complete the table below to capture the languages, religions and other cultural expressions brought to the Caribbean by any TWO groups that migrated to the region.

GROUP	LANGUAGE	RELIGION	OTHER CULTURAL EXPRESSIONS

6 Extended Learning

Project: Do you have a family member or neighbour who migrated outside of the Caribbean?

Conduct an interview with that person to find out:

– when they migrated

– the reason/s why they migrated

– THREE things they liked about the new country

– THREE things they missed about their Caribbean home.

7 Use the information on pages 20 and 21 of your atlas to help you complete this crossword.

Across

3. African group
5. Viking explorer
8. South American Country with oilfields
9. Carried captured persons overseas
12. Movement of people
14. Home to the city of Toronto
16. Country in Asia
17. City where Caribbean people emigrate
19. Ocean crossed by captured Africans
20. Migrants settled in Trinidad, Jamaica and Guyana

Down

1. Place Columbus first landed in 1492
2. Caribbean people emigrated between 1945–1962
4. Forced African labourers
6. Persons migrated to Suriname
7. Crossed 13,000 years ago
10. Amerindian group in South America
11. Built by Caribbean migrants help
13. Descendants live in Belize
15. Carib descendants live on this island
18. Migrated from South America

What are some of the environmental issues in the Caribbean?

1 What are some of the environmental issues affecting the countries below?

COUNTRY	ENVIRONMENTAL ISSUE
Belize	
Cayman Islands	
Jamaica	
Haiti	
Curacao	

2 On the map of the Caribbean that follows:

- Shade in blue, areas affected by invasive species

- Shade in green, areas with endangered species

- Shade in red, areas where pollution is an issue

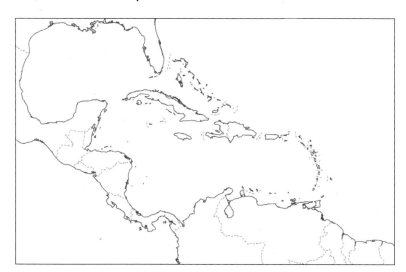

3 Discuss how you could help reduce environmental problems.

Decide on one thing you could do and outline it here.

What do you know about environmental problems in the Caribbean?

1 Choose THREE issues from pages 22 and 23 of your atlas.

2 Draw a picture of each issue. Write a few words about what may cause it to develop and how it may affect us.

Which islands make up The Bahamas?

1 Using page 24 of your atlas, label the islands listed in the panel on the map.

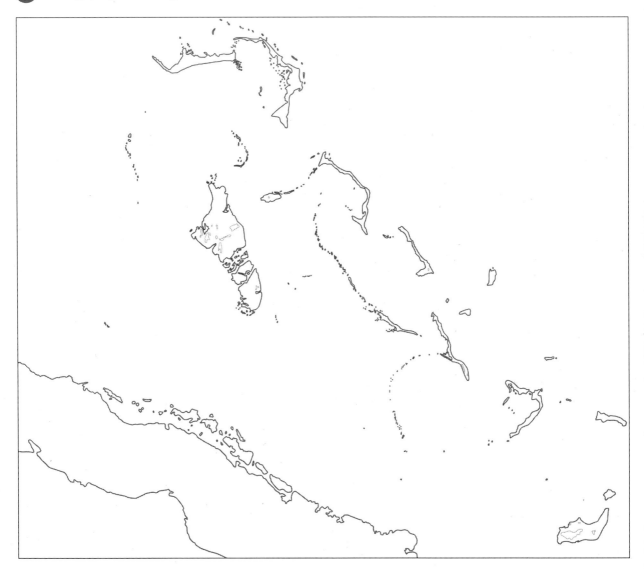

2 Can you guess the island?

    (a) I am on the Tropic of Cancer, east of Great Exuma. _____

    (b) I am home to the capital, Nassau. _____

    (c) This is where you will find Blue Holes National park. _____

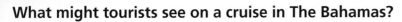

A Cruise in the Bahamas

What might tourists see on a cruise in The Bahamas?

1 **Plan a brief, four-day itinerary for a cruise ship.**

Write down which islands you might visit and state the things you may do there.

DAY	ISLAND	ACTIVITY
Day 1		
Day 2		
Day 3		
Day 4		

2 **Draw a sketch map showing the route you would take.**

Label the places where you will stop and name the main attractions.

3 **Add a title, key and compass to your map.**

What is the population in the Bahamas like?

1 List the FIVE islands in the Bahamas with the highest population.

Add data about the number of people and the population density.

ISLAND	POPULATION	DENSITY

2 Colour and label the islands with the most people on the map below.

3 Now answer these questions.

(a) Which island is the most crowded? _____

(b) When did the population start to grow rapidly? _____

(c) What pattern does your map show? _____

(d) Which are the most populated of the Turks and Caicos Islands?

_____

Which are the true statements about Cuba?

1 **Using page 26 of your atlas, find the answer to each of the statements below.**

Colour the circle green if you think it is TRUE and red if you think it is FALSE.

STATEMENT	TRUE	FALSE
1 The capital city of Cuba is Antiago De Cuba	○	○
2 The highest peak on Cuba is 1156 metres high	○	○
3 Guantanamo Bay is a US naval base	○	○
4 The wettest month in Havana is February	○	○
5 Cuba is approximately 1200 km from east to west	○	○
6 Cuba has four major resorts	○	○
7 Cuba lies to the south of The Bahamas	○	○
8 Fidel Castro ruled Cuba from 1959 to 2008	○	○
9 The national bird of Cuba is the brown pelican	○	○
10 Cuba was discovered by Columbus in 1792	○	○

2 **Now make up your own Cuba quiz with true or false statements.**

STATEMENT	TRUE	FALSE
	○	○
	○	○
	○	○
	○	○
	○	○
	○	○
	○	○
	○	○
	○	○
	○	○

What can you do in the Cayman Islands?

1 Complete the table below by adding this information.

(a) The names of the THREE Cayman Islands

(b) The population of each island

(c) The length of each island

NAME OF ISLAND	POPULATION	LENGTH (estimate)

2 Imagine you are a tourist visiting Grand Cayman. Where would you go to do the things listed below?

ACTIVITY	PLACE
Relax on beach	
Visit a museum	
See turtles	
Visit a garden	
Explore a cave	
See a coral reef	
See iguanas	

3 Which ONE activity would you most likely do and why?

What features does Jamaica have and where are they?

1 Complete the table below by adding the name of the feature from the map on pages 28 and 29 of the atlas.

DESCRIPTION	GRID SQUARE	NAME of FEATURE
A capital city	D1	
A bluff	B1	
A peak of 955 metres	B2	
A harbour	A2	
A mountain range	D2	
A river	E2	
An island	C1	
A bay near Governor's Hill	C2	

Finding places in Jamaica

2 In what direction are the following places from Kingston?

Portmore: _____

Port Antonio: _____

Morant Bay: _____

3 What is the distance between Kingston and the main airports?

Norman Manley International Airport: _____

Sansgter International Airport: _____

Ian Flemming International Airport: _____

4 Show and label all the features above on the blank map below.

5 Add areas of rainforest and bauxite mining using the map on page 32.

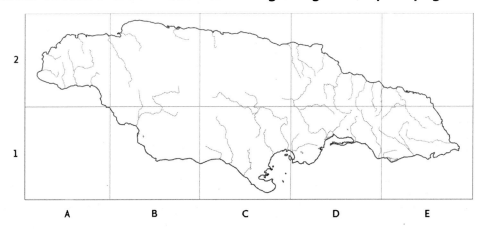

Jamaica climate

What is the climate of Jamaica like?

1. Using the map on pages 28 and 29 of the atlas, find the compass direction from Kingston to Port Antonio. _____

2. Using the rainfall charts on page 30, complete this table.

RAINFALL	PORT ANTONIO	KINGSTON
Months with <50 mm rainfall		
Months with >150 mm rainfall		
Rainfall in wettest month		
Rainfall in driest month		

3. What do you notice about the rainfall patterns in Port Antonio and Kingston?

4. State the direction of the predominant wind (see page 14). _____

5. Compare the climate map with the parishes map on page 28:

   – Which of the parishes has places that receive more than 3500 mm of rain?

   – Which parishes have places that receive between 3000 and 3500 mm of rain?

   – In which parishes are there places that receive less than 1000 mm of rain?

6. What crop is grown around Port Antonio that needs rain (see page 32)?

7. **Extended Learning**

   Why do you think Port Antonio receives so much more rain than Kingston? Discuss with your classmates and then use the internet to find out.

Reviewing the history, culture and tourism of Jamaica

1 Fill in the missing words in the sentences below.

(a) The _____ and the _____ peoples migrated from South America and settled in Jamaica.

(b) The _____ captured Jamaica from the Spanish in 1655. _____ _____ labour was used on plantation economies in Jamaica.

(c) Contract labour from _____ and _____ was used to work on plantations in Jamaica after Emancipation.

(d) _____ replaced sugar as Jamaica's main export by 1952.

(e) Jamaica gained its independence in the year _____.

2 Jamaican Music and Sports Journal entry

(a) Write in your journal THREE styles of music from Jamaica. State your favourite style and why you like it. Write a paragraph on the musical accomplishments of your favourite Jamaican artist. Add a picture of him or her in your journal.

(b) In your journal, paste pictures of Usain Bolt, Veronica Campbell Brown and Shelly-Ann Fraser. Browse the internet and write a paragraph on their sporting accomplishments.

(c) What is your favourite sport? Write a paragraph on why you like that sport and on your favourite sports person.

What do you know about the tourist industry in Jamaica?

Take a look at the graphs on Tourism on page 33 of your atlas and answer the following questions.

3 In which year did Jamaica record the most stop-over visitor arrivals? _____

4 What is the main purpose of the visit for stop-over visitor arrivals in Jamaica?

_____

5 Name the country that the most stop-over visitor arrivals to Jamaica came from.

_____

6 In what month of the year is the largest number of cruise ship passenger arrivals recorded? _____

What are the main features of Haiti and the Dominican Republic?

1 Complete the map below by adding and labelling the following features:

- – the capital city of each country

- – the border between the two countries

- – a lake, a mountain and a headland

- – a scale bar and north point

- – the highest peak in each country.

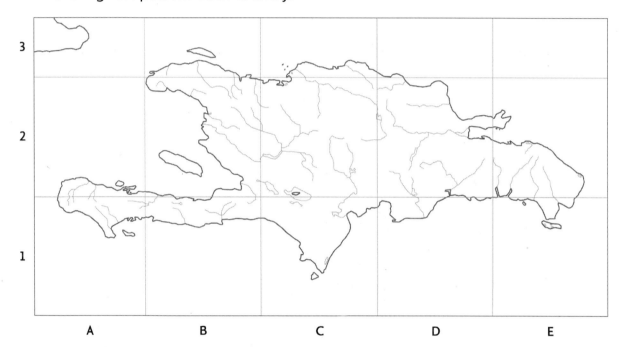

2 What is the distance between the two capital cities?

_____

3 Complete these sentences:

Haiti is _____ by area than the Dominican Republic.

The main language in Haiti is _____ or _____.

The country with the most national parks is the _____.

How have Haiti and the Dominican Republic changed over time?

1 Complete the timelines for THREE events in Haiti and THREE events in the Dominican Republic.

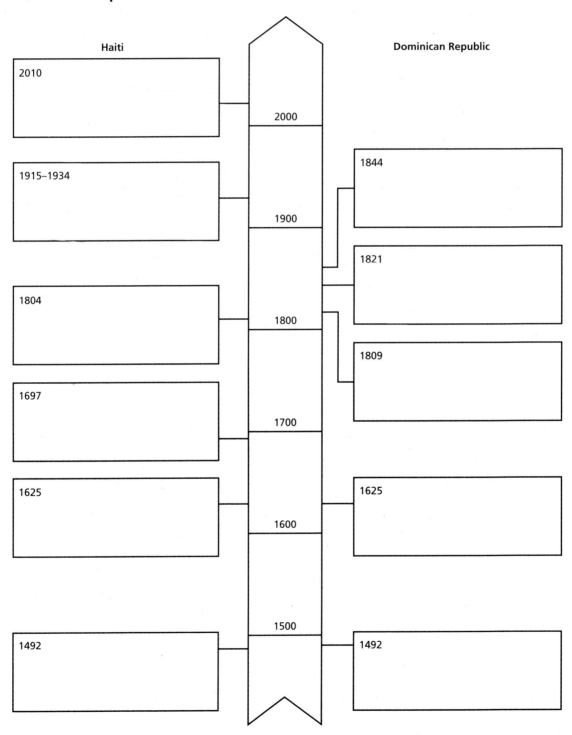

Haiti

| 2010 |

| 1915–1934 |

| 1804 |

| 1697 |

| 1625 |

| 1492 |

Dominican Republic

| 1844 |

| 1821 |

| 1809 |

| 1625 |

| 1492 |

2000

1900

1800

1700

1600

1500

What do you know about Puerto Rico?

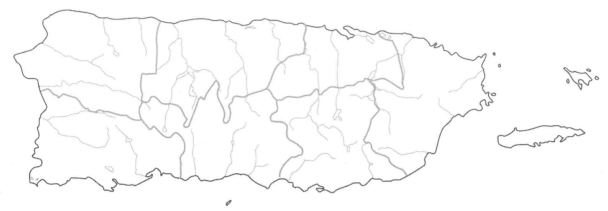

1 Using the map on page 35 of your atlas, label the districts shown on the map above.

2 Complete this simple fact file about Puerto Rico.

Population	
Capital city	
Area	
Highest mountain peak	
Main offshore island	
Main languages	
National animal	
Number of resorts	
Year of possession by the United States	

3 If you were visiting Puerto Rico, what TWO points of interest would you choose to visit and why?

_____

_____

_____

_____

US Virgin Islands

What are the US Virgin Islands like?

1 Name the THREE islands on the map below.

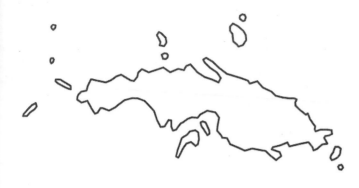

....

2 Complete this fact file about the US Virgin Islands.

Population	
Capital city	
Area	
Latitude	
Longitude	

3 Tell the story of the US Virgin Islands by filling in the gaps in the sentences below.

The islands were originally inhabited by the _____. Permanent settlement came when the _____ settled in St Thomas. Denmark bought St Croix from the _____ in _____. In 1917 Denmark sold the islands to the United States. The islands have many features. There include _____ Beach on St John's and _____ Distillery on St Croix.

50

Can you make a cube model of different Caribbean Islands?

1. Draw the outline shape of each of the islands named on a photocopy of the cube template.

2. Mark and name the capital towns.

3. Cut round the edge of the template.

4. Fold down the flaps and fold along the edge of each cube face.

5. Glue your cube together.

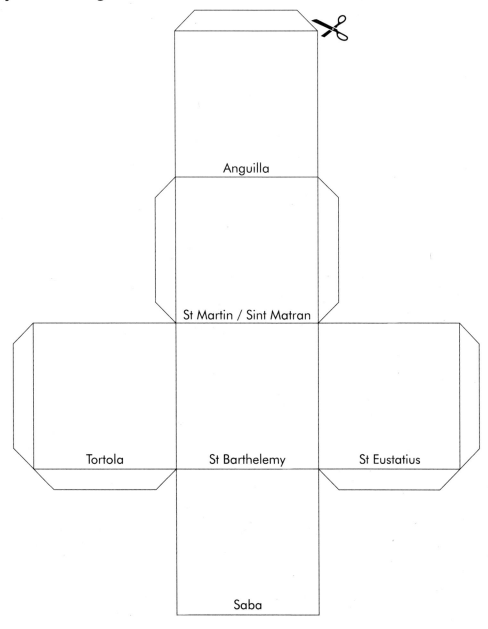

Caribbean Islands word search

Which island names do you know?

1 See if you can find these islands in the word search below.

Saba	St Martin	St Eustatius	Anguilla
Anegada	Tortola	Virgin	Garda
St Barthelemy	Sint Maarten	Ginger Island	Peter Island

E	M	S	T	E	U	S	T	A	T	I	U	S	O	P
S	S	A	R	N	A	N	G	U	I	L	L	A	J	X
W	J	A	T	G	N	F	H	O	E	L	Q	A	Z	K
B	S	C	O	J	E	O	G	W	B	E	A	V	U	P
V	T	B	R	A	G	F	C	P	R	S	C	A	M	E
O	M	S	T	B	A	R	T	H	E	L	E	M	Y	T
L	A	B	O	E	D	E	D	S	E	T	C	L	L	E
S	R	N	L	Q	A	E	W	V	D	P	R	P	O	R
E	T	W	A	C	N	S	X	Q	W	O	A	D	E	I
S	I	N	T	M	A	A	R	T	E	N	T	H	M	S
A	N	T	L	H	P	C	F	X	A	U	S	A	E	L
B	L	N	O	V	I	R	G	I	N	G	A	R	D	A
A	B	J	A	P	H	U	I	D	E	J	H	I	I	N
S	K	D	G	I	N	G	E	R	I	S	L	A	N	D
A	C	I	F	H	I	J	O	H	D	J	K	S	T	E

What is the landscape of St Kitts like?

1 How far is it across St Kitts from west to east along latitude 17°20′ N?

_____

2 Draw a cross section diagram across St Kitts at this line of latitude.

Use the map on page 37 and note especially the changes in contour height (green to yellow at 200 m and yellow to brown at 500 m).

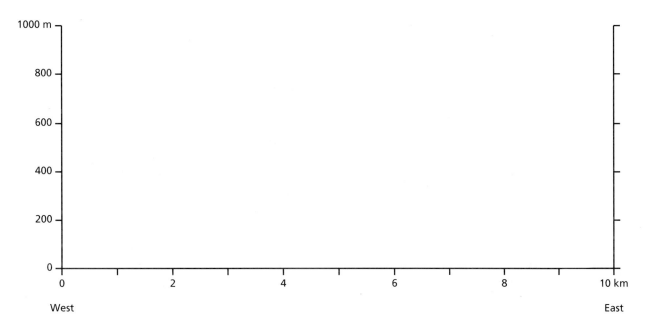

West   East

3 What do you notice about the roads leading northwest from Basseterre to Sandy Point Town?

_____

_____

4 What do you notice about the rivers in St Kitts?

_____

_____

What do names tell us about places in St Kitts and Nevis and in Montserrat?

1 Using the map on page 37 of your atlas, fill in the gaps in the table below.

PLACE NAME	ISLAND	FEATURE TYPE
Basseterre		
Soufriere Hills		
Nevis Peak		Highest peak
Trinity		District
	Montserrat	Capital town
	Nevis	Major resort
Parsons Gut	St Kitts	

Montserrat Case Study: 1995 Eruption

2 Use pages 17 and 37 of your atlas to add the following details on the map of Montserrat.

– Shade the areas that were covered by ash from the volcano.

– Insert the boundary line for the exclusion zone.

– Insert and label: the abandoned capital, the new capital and highest point in the safe zone.

3 Below are some feature names. Complete the tables by adding two examples for each of the place names that contain these words. Use the map on page 37.

BAY	

BLUFF	

CLIFF	

GHUT	

HILL	

POINT	

Antigua

What is Antigua like?

1 Add information about towns, roads, mountains and islands to this map of Antigua:

- the capital city and TWO important towns

- the main road from St John's to Cedar Grove and Willikies

- the names of its smaller islands

- shade areas over 200 m and add peaks.

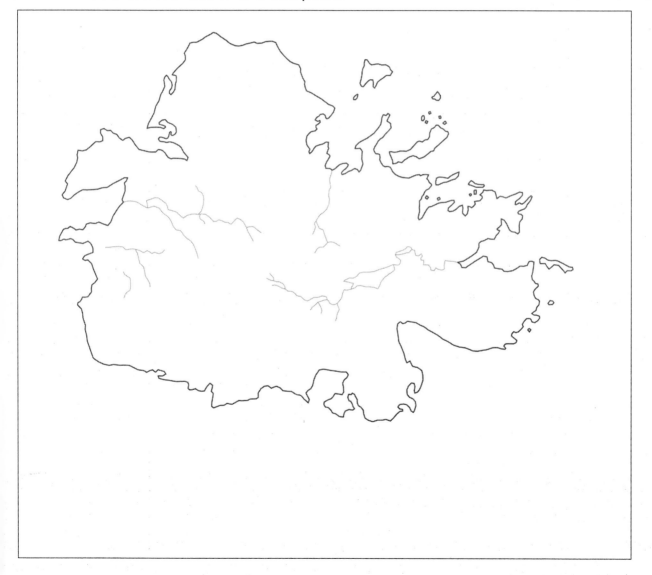

2 Add symbols and a key to show some other features.

What can you find out about Antigua and Barbuda?

1. Study page 38 of your atlas to find out about Antigua and Barbuda.

2. Now write a few sentences about each of the topics below.

HISTORY

SUGAR

WEATHER

TOURISM

Exploring Guadeloupe

What is the pattern of rainfall in Basse-Terre?

1 Using the figures from the table below, make a chart to show annual rainfall at Basse-Terre.

80	60	70	110	150	120	160	190	230	220	220	140
J	F	M	A	M	J	J	A	S	O	N	D

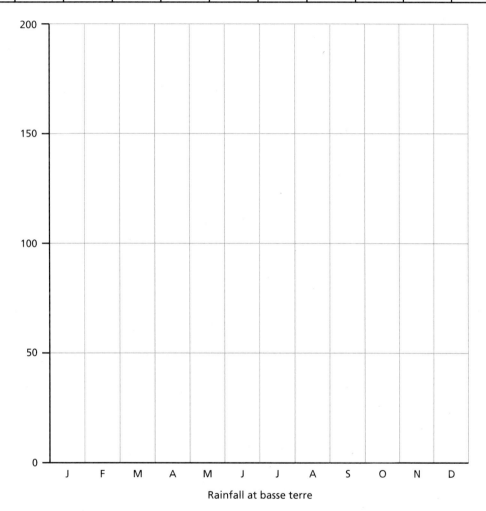

Rainfall at basse terre

2 What are the similarities and differences in rainfall between Basse-Terre and St Johns in Antigua? Can you think of the reasons for this?

_____

_____

_____

Exploring Dominica

1 Create a fact file about Dominica and its key features using the prompts below. Use the information on page 40 of the atlas to help you.

Island size: length and breadth	
Capital town	
Physical features	
Highest point	
National Parks	
Parish names	
Tourist attractions	
Wettest months	
Driest months	
Became a Republic in:	

2 Draw your own map of the island and add the information from your table above.

3 Both the French and the British colonised this island in the past. Can you find examples of English and French place names?

_____

_____

Mount Pelée

Why is Mount Pelée famous?

1 **Read the description of what happened at Mount Pelée in 1902.**

> ### Disaster in Martinique
>
> The eruption of Mount Pelée was the worst volcanic disaster of the twentieth century. In less than one minute the whole city of St Pierre was wiped out. In the days leading up to May 2, 1902 the volcano had been smoky and emitting vapours. Then it suddenly erupted. A gigantic mushroom cloud filled the sky and a cloud of ash surged over the city with temperatures over 500 degrees Centigrade. Some people burned to death on the spot. Others felt their blood start to boil. The city itself burst into flames. Only three people survived. Ones of them was a prisoner in solitary confinement in the town goal.

2 **Using the information and images from the internet, make up the front page for a newspaper reporting on the Mount Pelée disaster. The story should include a map showing Mount Pelée, St Pierre and the capital city. Start by drawing your map here.**

Where do people live in St Lucia?

1 **Mark these settlements and other features on a map of St Lucia.**

Capital city:

Castries

Important towns:

Anes-la-Raye

Canaries

Choiseul

Dennery

Gros Islet

Laborie

Micoud

Soufrière

Vieux Fort

Areas of volcanic activity:

Gros Piton

Petit Piton

The two national parks

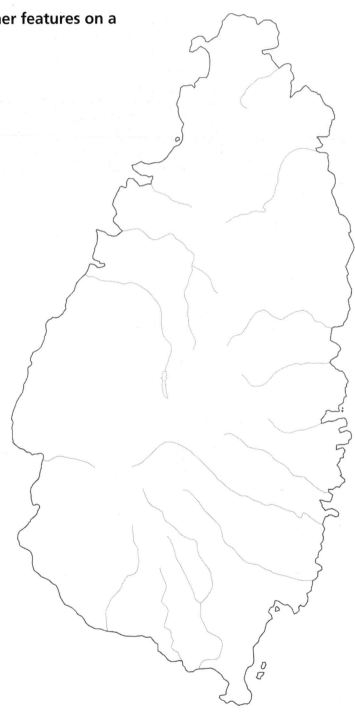

2 **Draw the road that links the settlements together.**

3 **What is similar about all the settlements?**

4 **Where do least people live?**

What are the main islands in St Vincent and the Grenadines?

1 Working from page 42 of your atlas, label the islands shown on this map.

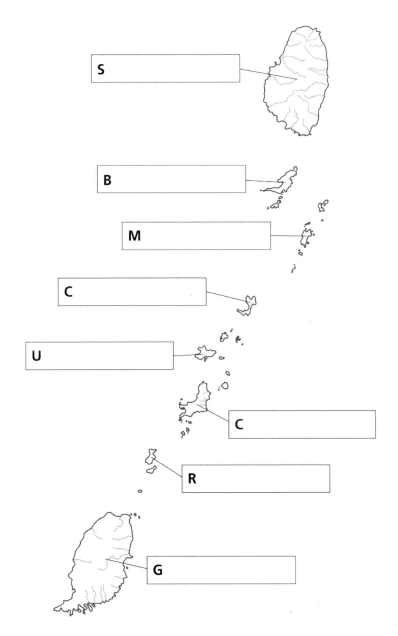

S

B

M

C

U

C

R

G

2 Add Kingstown and St George's to your map.

3 Approximately how far is it by boat between the two cities? _____

4 If you set out from Kingstown, what compass direction would you need to take to get to St George's? _____

Spice island

What spices are grown on Grenada?

1 Complete the spice word ladder, using page 43 of your atlas to help you.

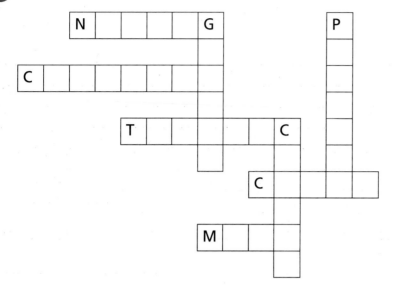

2 **(a)** Using the information about other Caribbean islands in your atlas, find out the percentages of economic activity given over to agriculture, fishing, and forestry in different places.

ISLAND	PERCENTAGE
Grenada	
Barbados	
Guadaloupe	
St Kitts and Nevis	

(b) Can you explain these differences?

_____

_____

_____

_____

Barbados economic activity

How do people make a living in Barbados?

1 Look carefully at page 45 of your atlas and write some useful facts about these industries.

FISHING
•
•
•

SUGAR
•
•
•

TOURISM
•
•
•

RUM
•
•
•

2 Show some of the places which are linked to these industries on the map opposite.

3 Use a key to indicate the industry links.

Key

INDUSTRY	SYMBOL

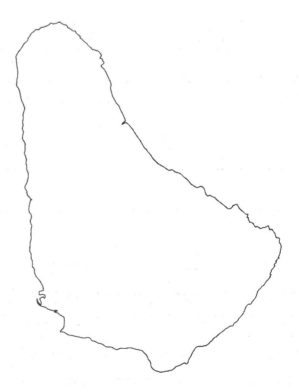

We do you know about Barbados?

1 See if you can find TEN words about Barbados in this word search. They are all on page 45 of your atlas.

D	U	H	C	M	R	Q	U	B	A	H	T
A	P	F	I	S	H	I	N	G	J	L	O
C	E	A	R	A	W	A	K	U	E	R	B
F	O	R	G	O	S	W	I	F	R	C	A
K	I	L	T	I	F	G	P	U	O	L	C
C	R	E	O	L	C	B	M	Z	S	E	C
D	X	W	Y	N	S	J	E	T	T	R	O
U	X	F	L	E	Y	B	R	K	G	C	R
S	C	O	T	T	O	N	P	O	D	E	V
I	F	E	Y	L	D	S	S	U	G	A	R
H	T	O	U	R	I	S	M	U	T	A	D
E	F	A	K	O	O	L	P	H	I	N	B

2 Write a brief description about Barbados using the words you found in the word search.

_____

_____

_____

_____

_____

_____

_____

_____

What is special about Aruba, Benaire and Curacao?

1 Name each island and mark its capital town.

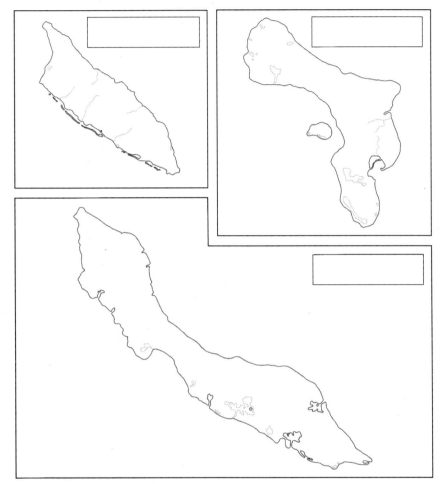

2 Add ONE feature to each island to do with the oil industry.

3 What else makes these islands special? State THREE facts about them.

What are the true statements about Trinidad and Tobago?

1 Using pages 47–51 of your atlas, find the answer to each of the statements below. Colour the circle green if you think it is true and red if you think it is false.

STATEMENT	TRUE	FALSE
1 Port of Spain is the capital city of Trinidad.	○	○
2 Icacos has less rainfall than Cumaca.	○	○
3 The highest point in Tobago, Centre Hill, is 765 m high.	○	○
4 The Pitch Lake is the world's largest deposit of mud.	○	○
5 Crown Point is the at the southwestern tip of Tobago.	○	○
6 Tourism makes up 42% of the economic activity in Trinidad.	○	○
7 The Caroni Swamp is located on the east coast of Trinidad.	○	○
8 In the past, immigrants have come to Trinidad and Tobago from St Helena.	○	○
9 Devil's Woodyard mud volcano has been active for over 150 years.	○	○
10 It is less than 20 km from Trinidad to Venezuela.	○	○

2 Now make up your own quiz of true/false statements.

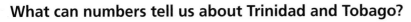

Trinidad and Tobago in numbers

What can numbers tell us about Trinidad and Tobago?

1. Working from page 51 of your atlas, draw a bar graph showing the flow of people into Trinidad and Tobago.

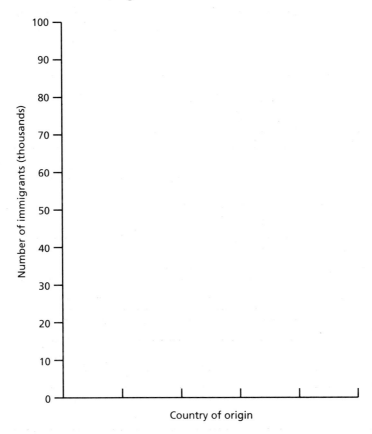

2. Working from pages 50 and 51, complete the table below.

Date when slavery was abolished	
Date when Trinidad and Tobago gained independence	
Percentage of economic activity that comes from petroleum	
The annual benefit from tourism in US dollars	
The approximate number of stop-over visitor arrivals in 2014	
The number of additional visitors attracted by carnival	

Rain shadow

Why are some parts of Tobago much wetter than others?

1. Using the map of Tobago on page 53 of your atlas, complete the cross-section diagram below.

2. Begin by naming Buccoo in the southwest and Charlotteville in the northeast. Add labels for the Centre Hill and Main Ridge.

3. Put dots at the correct points to show the height of Centre Hill and the edge of Main Ridge.

4. Now join the dots to complete the cross section.

5. Add drawings of cloud and rain over Charlotteville and Main Ridge.

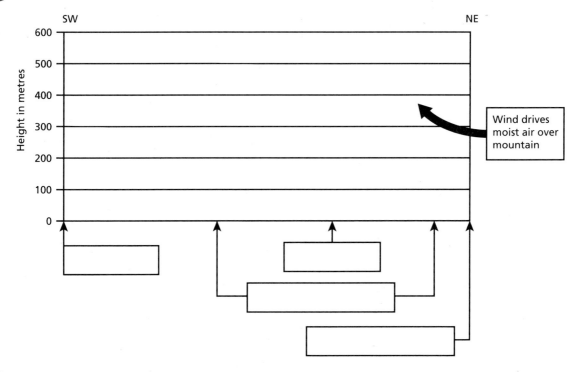

6. **Extended Learning**

Why is Charlotteville so much wetter than Buccoo? Use the internet to find out what you can.

What are the places of interest in Trinidad?

1 You will need two dice for this activity.

2 Throw the dice, add up the numbers and colour the correct circle in the table.

3 Stop when you have coloured SIX circles.

4 Now mark the places you are going to visit on the map.

1 Carib Brewery	2 River Estate Waterwheel	3 Cedros Bay	4 Toco Lighthouse	5 Fort George	6 La Brea Pitch Lake
○	○	○	○	○	○
7 Nariva Swamp	8 Aripo Caves	9 Piparo Mud Volcano	10 Temple in the Sea	11 Caroni Swamp	12 Bush Bush Wildlife Sanctuary
○	○	○	○	○	○

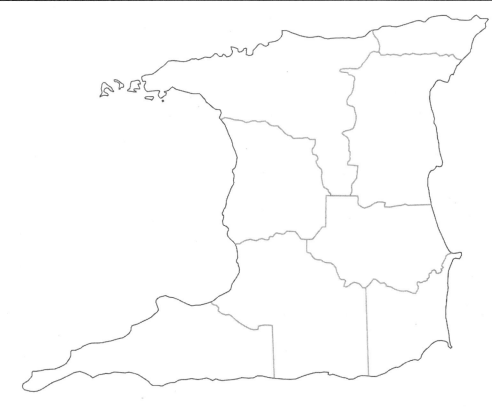

5 Draw a line showing the best route for your mystery tour.

1 **Fill in the blanks.**

1. In the year _____ Trinidad passed from _____ rule to _____ rule.

2. In the year 1976 Trinidad and Tobago became a _____.

3. _____ is Trinidad's main social and cultural event.

4. In 2014, the month of _____ recorded the most stop over visitor arrivals to Trinidad.

5. Thirty-nine per cent of Trinidad's visitors came from the _____.

2 **Extended Learning**

Form a group of 4–6 people.

Play via YouTube or CD or other media device a piece of music or song on the steel band.

Write down your reaction to the music in your journal.

Browse the internet or your school library and write a paragraph on the origins of steel band.

3 Find the following words in the word search grid:

ARAWAK   BRITISH   CARIB   CARNIVAL   CELEBRATION   COLONISED
CROWN COLONY   CULTURAL   EASTERN CARIBBEAN   EMANCIPATION
EXPENDITURE   FESTIVAL   IMMIGRANTS   INDEPENDENCE   INDIGENOUS
LENT   MADERIA   MIGRATION   PLANTATIONS   REPUBLIC
SLAVERY   SYRIA   TOBAGO   TOURIST   TRINIDAD

C	I	N	N	C	Q	N	Z	K	K	O	D	W	I	Y	J	G	E
U	N	H	O	M	R	M	O	A	F	A	V	M	S	O	D	A	U
L	D	S	I	I	L	O	W	I	D	E	M	U	S	L	S	D	T
T	I	I	T	C	T	A	W	I	T	I	S	N	F	T	G	O	L
U	G	T	A	U	R	A	N	N	G	A	O	T	E	B	U	V	A
R	E	I	R	A	Y	I	P	R	C	I	R	R	I	R	G	J	V
A	N	R	B	C	R	R	A	I	T	O	N	G	I	V	W	W	I
L	O	B	E	T	A	N	E	A	C	C	L	S	I	L	A	R	N
S	U	R	L	K	T	R	T	V	A	N	T	O	E	M	Z	L	R
Y	S	I	E	S	V	N	I	R	A	U	A	N	N	X	Y	G	A
R	U	D	C	P	A	J	I	B	P	L	T	M	I	Y	L	D	C
I	R	F	V	L	C	B	T	M	O	L	S	L	E	N	H	Q	S
A	M	M	P	A	B	E	X	P	E	N	D	I	T	U	R	E	U
P	E	C	N	E	D	N	E	P	E	D	N	I	G	V	M	T	R
T	O	B	A	G	O	G	G	I	D	E	S	I	N	O	L	O	C
J	C	N	E	I	F	R	E	P	U	B	L	I	C	I	Q	R	H
C	O	R	I	X	R	C	B	B	A	I	R	E	D	A	M	I	Y
B	K	H	C	T	I	X	P	Q	U	K	R	W	Y	R	U	Y	U

4 Choose SIX words from the word search and make sentences with them. Write them here and share with the class.

_____

_____

_____

_____

What do you know about Guyana?

1 Complete the fact file about the physical geography of Guyana using page 54 of your atlas.

PHYSICAL GEOGRAPHY	
Highest mountain	
Longest river (starts with letter 'E')	
Length north-south (see page 11)	
Width east-west (see page 11)	
Wettest month (Georgetown)	

2 Complete this fact file about the human geography of Guyana using pages 54 and 11 of your atlas.

HUMAN GEOGRAPHY	
Capital city	
Surrounding countries	
Province claimed by Suriname	
Province claimed by Venezuela	

3 Examine the lower right photograph on page 55 of your atlas.

(a) What activity is being carried out in the photograph?

_____

(b) Use the map on page 54 to name the provinces in which this activity occurs.

_____

(c) From the photograph, what impact is this activity having on the environment?

_____

4 **Extended Learning**

What do you know about the border dispute between Guyana and Venezuela? Find out what you can about this dispute by researching on the internet.

The River Essequibo

What is the River Essequibo like?

1 Add these labels to the map of the River Essequibo.

(a) Atlantic Ocean, where the river empties

(b) Pakaraima Mountains, found west of the river

(c) Amuka Mts, where the river begins

(d) River Mazaruni and River Cuyuni, two of its tributaries

(e) Rappu Falls, one of its many waterfalls

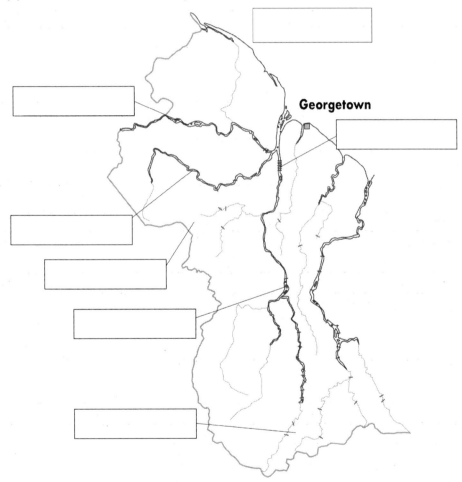

Georgetown

2 Extended Learning

Use the internet to find out what you might see on an expedition up the River Essequibo.

Think about plants and creatures as well as physical geography.

What features can you find in different atlas map grid squares?

1 Using page 54 of your atlas, write down one feature you found in each grid square.

GRID SQUARE	FEATURE	RIGHT/WRONG
A4		
B4		
C4		
A3		
B3		
C3		
B2		
C2		

2 Find a partner and ask them to name the grid square for each feature.

3 Check if they were right or wrong.

4 Now choose one grid square which you think looks particularly interesting. Say why you selected it.

My grid square is _____

What makes it interesting?

_____

_____

_____

_____

_____

_____

_____

1 What is most interesting or important about Belize? You will need to work in groups of two or three for this activity.

(a) Using a photocopy of this page, cut out the fact cards about Belize and place them on the table in front of you.

(b) Now put the fact cards in 'diamond ranking' order. Put the most important or interesting fact at the top, the two most important on the second row and so on.

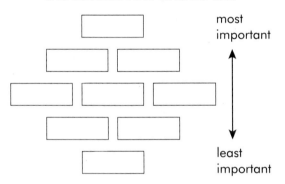

(c) Keep moving the fact cards until you all agree.

(d) See if other pupils in your class have the same opinion.

Physical features of Belize

2 Write the name(s) of the following features.

- TWO lagoons _____ _____
- ONE mountain _____
- ONE plateau _____
- TWO rivers   _____ _____
- ONE hill   _____
- TWO bays   _____ _____

FACTS ABOUT BELIZE

Belize was once home to the ancient Mayan civilization.
The rainforest cover is in decline.
An underwater cave, the Great Blue Hole, attracts many tourists.
The western frontier follows a line of longitude.
The coral barrier reef is home to many plants and animals.
Chewing gum was once made from trees found in Belize.
Belize was once a British colony.
Over half the population speaks both English and Spanish.
Belize is sometimes hit by hurricanes.

What can you learn from a map of Central America?

1 Label the countries on the map below.

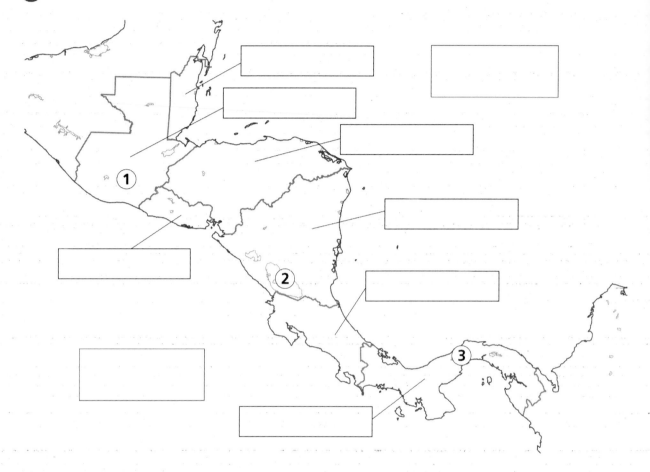

2 Add labels for the Pacific Ocean and Caribbean Sea.

3 Find out from the physical features map on page 57 of your atlas what each number shows.

① _____

② _____

③ _____

4 Which of these THREE features do you think is most important?

_____

What can you say about Central America?

1 **Complete the sentences below.**

(a)   Nicaragua is the _____ country in Central America.

(b)   Belize has a land border to the west with _____.

(c)   El Salvador has a coast on the _____.

(d)   Panama is _____ 10 degrees north of the Equator.

(e)   The Maya Mountains are in _____ and _____.

(f)   _____ is the largest city in Central America.

(g)   Honduras is _____ than El Salvador.

(h)   Coast Rica lies to the _____ of Nicaragua.

(i)   The Panama Canal links the Caribbean Sea and the _____.

(j)   It is around 600 km from the west to the east of _____.

2 **Now make up FIVE more sentences of your own about Central America.**

Which are the different cities in North America?

1 **(a)** Using the map on page 58, name a city in each of these grid squares.

GRID SQUARE	CITY	GRID SQUARE	CITY
J4		K5	
G7		E9	
L6		H8	
M7		I5	
J6		N8	

(b) Name the cities which are in the Tropics.

_____

(c) Name the cities which are more than 60° north.

_____

(d) Name the cities which are exactly:

    (i) 30° north _____

    (ii) 50° north _____

    (iii) 80° west _____

What are some of the physical features of North America?

1 Using the maps on pages 58 and 59, complete the tables below.

MOUNTAINS	COUNTRY	HEIGHT
Volcan Popocatepetl		
Denali		
Mount Elbert		

RIVER	SEA OR OCEAN IT FLOWS INTO
Mississippi	
St Lawrence	
Colorado	

ISLAND	COUNTRY IT IS PART OF
Newfoundland	
Baffin Island	
Greenland	

LAKE	ON USA/CANADA BORDER

2 Write about some of the other physical features of North America.

What is the shape of different countries in South America?

1 Using page 60 of your atlas, find the countries which match each shape.

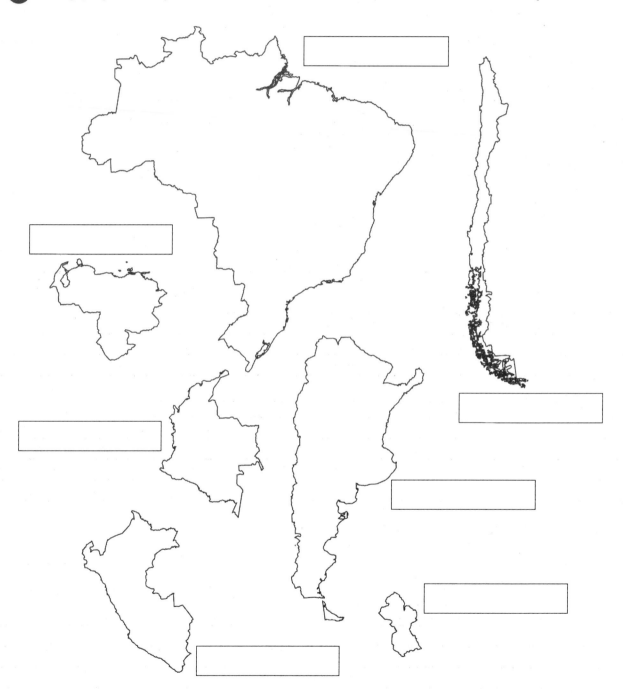

2 Now complete the country labels.

3 Name FOUR other South American countries. _____

What are the capital cities in South America?

1 Name the capital cities shown on the map.

2 Put a star next to the cities which are near or on the coast.

3 What are some benefits of locating along the coast?

_____

What can you show on a map of Africa?

1 Draw symbols to complete the key.

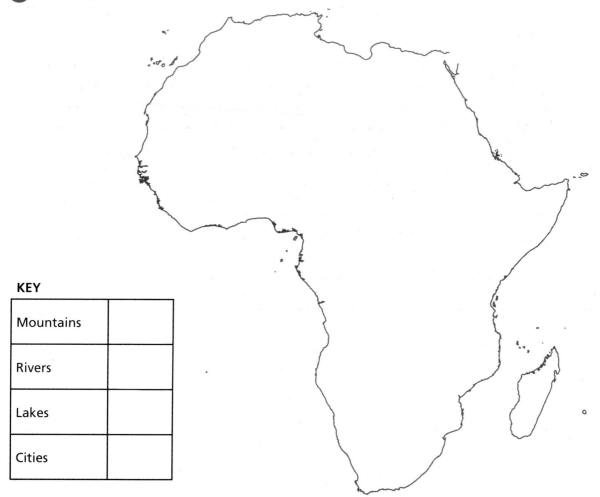

KEY

Mountains	
Rivers	
Lakes	
Cities	

2 Add a north point to your map.

3 Insert and name these features:

Mountain peaks: Kilimanjaro, Ras Dejan, Ibel Toubkal

Rivers: Nile, Niger, Zambezi

Lakes: Victoria

Line of latitude: Equator

Cities: Cairo, Lagos, Cape Town

Africa countries game

PHOTOCOPIABLE PAGE

1 **What are the capital cities in Africa?**

(a) Working in small groups (2–4) cut out the country name cards. Use a photocopy of this page.

(b) Place the cards face down in front of you.

(c) Turn the cards over one by one.

(d) The first person to name the capital city takes the card.

(e) When all the cards have gone, count up who has most.

Algeria	Nigeria	Egypt	Morocco	Kenya
Ghana	Uganda	Sudan	Tanzania	Zimbabwe
Democratic Republic of the Congo	Angola	South Africa	Libya	Zambia

2 **Complete the table below.**

OTHER FACTS ABOUT AFRICA	PLACE
Largest country	
Country with the largest population	
Countries with disputed borders	
Longest river	
Highest peak	
Largest desert	

How do grid squares help you find places?

1 Using the map on page 64, name a country in each of these grid squares.

D5		G6	
H5		E4	
G3		H3	
F6		G5	
C6		F4	

2 Using the map of page 65, give the grid square reference for these physical features.

Black Sea		Caucasus Mountains	
Mt Blanc		Mt Etna	
North Sea		Bay of Biscay	
River Rhone		Lake Ladoga	

3 Now write down the grid square references for different capital cities. Ask another pupil in your class to find them. Write down the answers when you both agree.

How are journeys effected by barriers?

1 Measure the distances between the cities to find out far it is from Lisbon to Athens.

JOURNEY	DISTANCE
Lisbon–Madrid	
Madrid–Andorra	
Andorra–Ljubljana	
Ljubljana–Belgrade	
Belgrade–Athens	
TOTAL	

2 How many countries would you pass through on this journey? _____

3 Name TWO rivers and TWO mountain ranges you would cross.

RIVER	MOUNTAIN

4 Now find out the distance from Moscow to Dublin in the same way.

JOURNEY	DISTANCE
Moscow–Vilnus	
Vilnus–Berlin	
Berlin–Amsterdam	
Amsterdam–Dublin	
TOTAL	

5 How many countries would you pass through on this journey? _____

6 Name TWO rivers and TWO seas you would have to cross.

RIVER	SEA

7 Discuss the barriers which you think are hardest to cross.

What are the names of the different countries in Asia?

1 Compile the A–Z of Asian countries below.

Leave out D, E, H, W, X and Z as there are no Asian countries starting with these letters.

2 Put a star next to any letters with more than one country name.

A		N	
B		O	
C		P	
D		Q	
E		R	
F		S	
G		T	
H		U	
I		V	
J		W	
K		X	
L		Y	
M		Z	

3 Imagine you have been asked to invent names for new countries to fill the empty spaces. What would they be?

Asia physical features

What are some of the main physical features of Asia?

1 Using the maps on page 66 and 67, complete the tables below.

MOUNTAIN PEAK	HEIGHT	MOUNTAIN RANGE
Mount Everest		
Elbrus		
Gora Narodnaya		

RIVER	SEA IT FLOWS INTO
Indus	
Chang Jiang	
Ob	
Mekong	
Ganges	

DESERT	COUNTRY WHERE IT IS FOUND
Gobi	
Thar	
Rub' al Khali	

ISLAND	COUNTRY IT BELONGS TO
Borneo	
Honshu	
Luzon	
Novaya Zemlya	

Oceania - latitude and longitude

What is the latitude and longitude of places in Oceania?

1 Label Australia, Papua New Guinea, New Zealand and Fiji on the map. Insert their capitals.

Also label: The Great Barrier Reef, Blue Mountains, Indian Ocean and Pacific Ocean

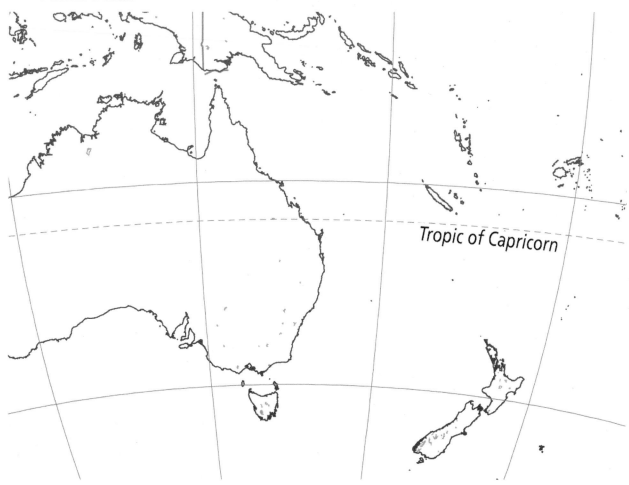

Tropic of Capricorn

2 Which lines of longitude pass through Australia? _____

3 Which capital city has a longitude of 160 degrees east? _____

4 Which line of latitude passes close to Wellington in New Zealand? _____

5 Which city lies on the Tropic of Capricorn? _____

Are all islands the same?

1 Using pages 68 and 69 of your atlas, fill in the gaps in the sentences below.

2 Make drawings in the empty boxes to go with the writing.

The capital city of Tuvalu is _____.
Tuvalu is made is made up of
_____reefs. These are only a few
_____high. If sea levels rise, they
could _____. The _____
are also coral islands.

The capital city of _____is Suva.
Fiji is made up of volcanic _____.
The highest is _____ metres high.
_____and _____are also
volcanic islands.

Antarctica

What is Antarctica like?

1 Complete the map of Antarctica by marking these features.

South Pole   Antarctic peninsula   Transantarctic mountains

Weddel Sea   Ross Sea   Mount Erebus

2 Add a scale bar.

3 Make a collection of photographs of Antarctica from the internet.

Which are the world's largest countries?

1 Look at the countries listed on the next page. Write the number of each country in the correct place on the map and colour the country shapes.

Canada ①   USA ②   Brazil ③

China ④   India ⑤   UK ⑥

Australia ⑦   Algeria ⑧   Russia ⑨

Democratic Republic of Congo ⑩   Argentina ⑪   Iran ⑫

2 **Name ONE very large country in each continent.**

Africa	
Asia	
North America	
South America	

Can you recognise different countries by their shape?

1. Use a photocopy of this page. Working with a partner, colour and cut out TWO sets of cards. You will each need to use the same colours.

2. Place the cards face down in front of you (24 in all).

3. Each player turns over a card then turns it back again in turn.

4. If you find a pair you take the cards and have another turn.

5. The winner is the person who collects the most pairs.

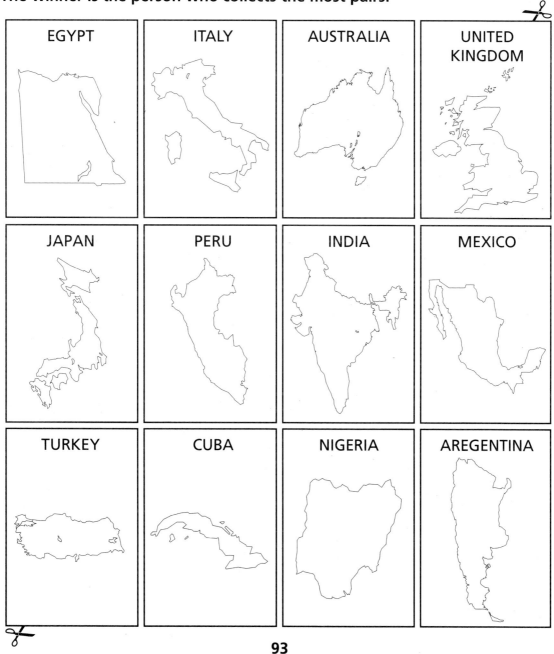

EGYPT	ITALY	AUSTRALIA	UNITED KINGDOM
JAPAN	PERU	INDIA	MEXICO
TURKEY	CUBA	NIGERIA	AREGENTINA

How do the continents compare in size?

1 The table tells you the size of each continent in million square kilometres.

Europe	11	Africa	30
North America	24	Oceania	9
South America	18	Antarctica	14
Asia	44		

Using this information, name and colour the shapes below.

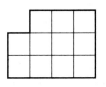

_____

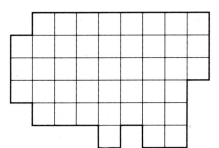

_____

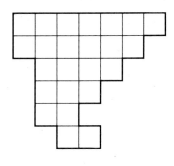

_____

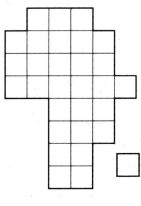

_____

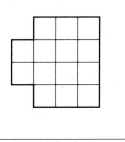

_____

_____

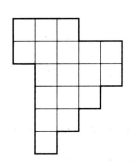

_____

_____

2 Name the TWO largest continents: _____ and _____

3 Name the TWO smallest continents: _____ and _____

Mountains

Which are the highest mountain peaks in each continent?

1 Working from pages 74 and 75 of your atlas, complete the table below.

MOUNTAIN PEAK	HEIGHT (m)	CONTINENT
Mt Everest		
Mt Blanc		
Denali		
K2		
Puncak Jaya		
Cerro Aconcagua		
Kilimanjaro		
Mount Cook		

2 Draw and name four mountains of your choice on the chart below.

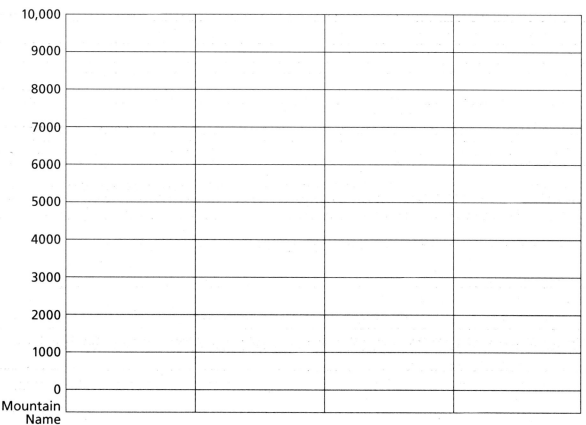

How do climates differ?

1 Using page 76 of your atlas, complete the fact files about the different climates.

TROPICAL
Description _____
_____
Atlas example _____
Minimum temperature _____
Maximum temperature _____
Rainfall pattern_____
_____

DESERT
Description _____
_____
Atlas example _____
Minimum temperature _____
Maximum temperature _____
Rainfall pattern_____
_____

SUBARCTIC
Description _____
_____
Atlas example _____
Minimum temperature _____
Maximum temperature _____
Rainfall pattern_____
_____

TEMPERATE
Description _____
_____
Atlas example _____
Minimum temperature _____
Maximum temperature _____
Rainfall pattern_____
_____

2 What is the climate type in your area?

_____

What is the pattern of winds around the world?

1 Label the eight points on the compass below.

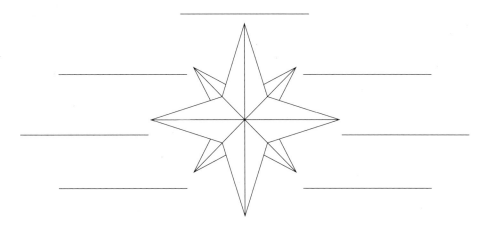

_____

_____   _____

_____   _____

_____   _____

_____

2 Using page 76 of your atlas, add arrows and name the winds on the globe diagram.

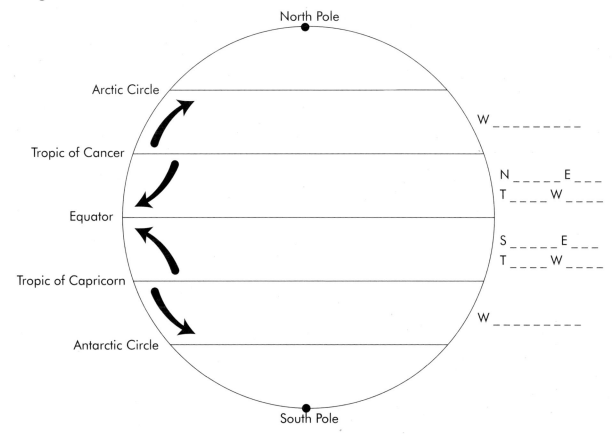

North Pole

Arctic Circle

W _ _ _ _ _ _ _ _

Tropic of Cancer

N _ _ _ _ _   E _ _ _
T _ _ _ _   W _ _ _ _

Equator

S _ _ _ _ _   E _ _ _
T _ _ _ _   W _ _ _ _

Tropic of Capricorn

W _ _ _ _ _ _ _ _

Antarctic Circle

South Pole

3 What type of wind is most common in the Caribbean? _____

What are the main types of vegetation around the world?

1 Write the words from the table in the correct fact files.

2 Colour the code boxes using the same colours as your atlas.

DESERT	TROPICAL FOREST	GRASSLAND	TUNDRA
sunny	hot	mild	ice
hot	wet	wet	snow
dry	misty	windy	frost
cacti	tall trees	shrubs	mosses

DESERT
Colour Code ☐

_____

_____

_____

_____

TROPICAL FOREST
Colour Code ☐

_____

_____

_____

_____

GRASSLAND
Colour Code ☐

_____

_____

_____

_____

TUNDRA
Colour Code ☐

_____

_____

_____

_____

3 Draw each animal named below in the empty right-hand box in the correct fact file.

(camel)   (parrot)   (squirrel)   (polar bear)

4 Extended Learning
Find out about other animals which live in different belts using the internet.

In the tropical forest

What is the tropical forest like?

1 Complete these sentences using the information given in the diagram on the right.

   (a) The tallest trees are over
          _____ high.

   (b) The forest floor is _____
          and _____.

   (c) In the shadowy layer plants
          _____
          _____.

   (d) There are many different
          _____ in the tropical
          forest.

2 Make drawings of the following different creatures on the diagram. Use the empty boxes for your drawings.

Tree canopy: toucan, monkey

Shadowy layer: boa constrictor (snake)

Forest floor: butterfly

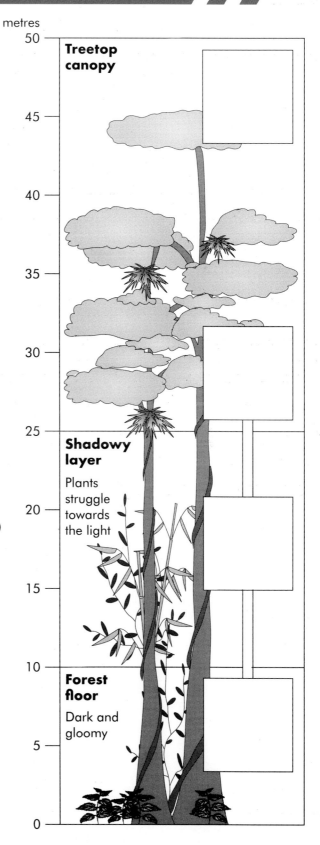

metres

Treetop canopy

Shadowy layer

Plants struggle towards the light

Forest floor

Dark and gloomy

Moving plates

What causes volcanoes?

1 Working from page 78 of your atlas, label and colour the magma, plates, lava and volcanoes on the diagrams below.

2 Under each diagram, write an explanation of what it shows.

Diverging plates

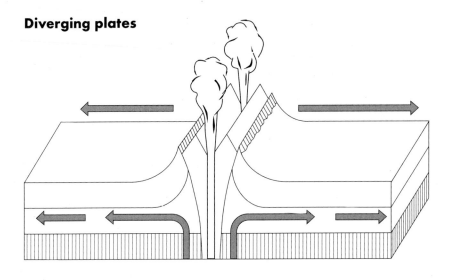

_____

_____

_____

Converging plates

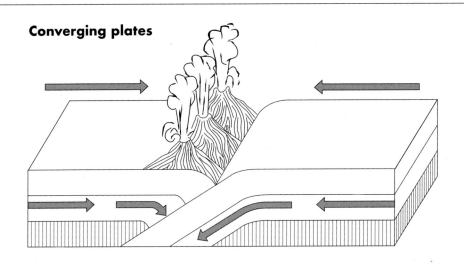

_____

_____

_____

What can you learn about different natural hazards?

> **Brain Teaser**
> What is a hazard? Can you name types of hazards?

1 See if you can find these words in the wordsearch.

earthquake	hazard
volcano	flood
stress	magma
plate	boundary
wave	crust
current	ridge

C	P	W	A	V	E	N	A	F	F	K	C
U	X	A	R	E	S	P	L	A	T	E	R
R	V	R	I	D	G	E	S	B	J	A	U
R	V	O	Z	U	O	T	M	H	B	R	S
E	N	O	L	E	Y	G	V	L	O	T	T
N	S	O	L	C	G	W	E	A	U	H	I
T	T	A	X	C	L	N	P	R	N	Q	S
S	R	I	C	H	A	Z	A	R	D	U	R
G	E	Y	O	R	T	N	O	H	A	A	S
A	S	F	L	O	O	D	O	E	R	K	I
K	S	Z	T	R	S	G	H	U	Y	E	O
E	K	S	M	A	G	M	A	P	C	U	M

2 Choose THREE of these words and write a sentence or two about how they are linked to hazards.

3 Examine the World Hazards map on pages 78 and 79.

    (a) Name the countries that are affected by annual flooding. _____

    (b) Name the country in the Caribbean which experienced flooding that caused over 1000 deaths in a year. _____ v

    (c) Which continent seems unaffected by earthquake and volcano hazards?
    _____

4 Compare with physical map of the world on pages 74 and 75 to identify rivers that experience major flooding.

_____

What are the different threats to the environment?

1 **Rate each of the problems in the table below, using a score from 1 to 5.**

You can use each number as much as you like.

Score: 1 = not very serious at all; 5 = very serious indeed.

PROBLEM	SCORE	PROBLEM	SCORE
Forest fires		Extreme weather	
Air pollution		Desertification	
Floods		Loss of wildlife	
Soil loss		Warming oceans	

2 **Join the correct points on the 'desire line' line diagram to show your opinion.**

Do other pupils in your class think the same?

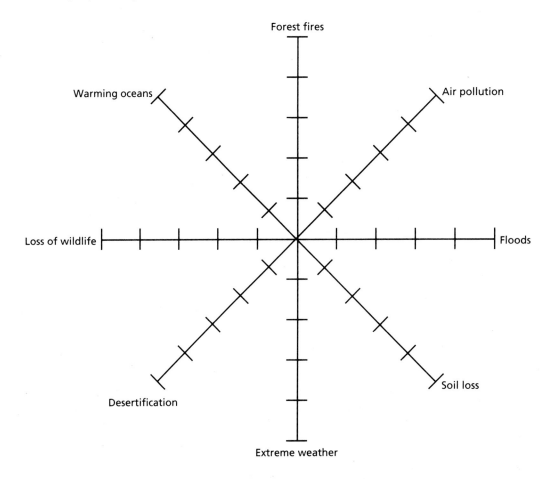

How can you make a model showing environmental issues?

1 **Make a 'picture tower' about environmental issues.**

(a) Draw a picture in each panel and say what is happening in a few words.

(b) Using a photocopy of this page, cut round the edges, fold along the dotted lines and glue the tower together.

Desertification	Deforestation	Pollution

Which is the largest city in each continent?

1 Working from pages 58–68 of your atlas, write down the population of the largest city in each continent to the nearest million.

CITY	POPULATION
Mexico City	
Sao Paulo	
Lagos	
Istanbul	
Tokyo	
Sydney	

2 Draw a block/bar graph to show this data. Label each column.

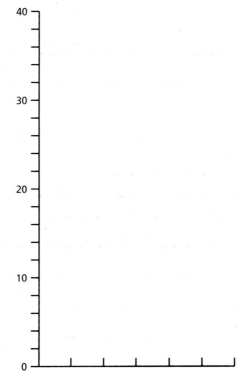

3 Discuss what else you know about city populations.

Mega cities

Which are the world's mega cities?

1 Using pages 82 and 83 to help you, mark these cities on the map below.

Beijing	New York	Sao Paulo	Tokyo
Delhi	Shanghai	Mumbai	Mexico City

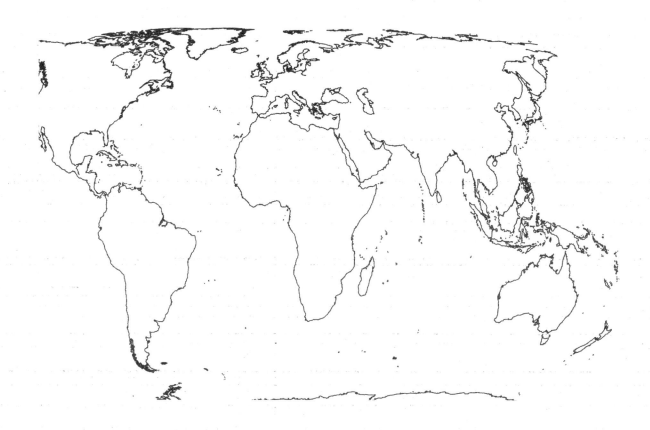

2 Which continent has the most large cities? _____

3 Which continents have no very large cities? _____

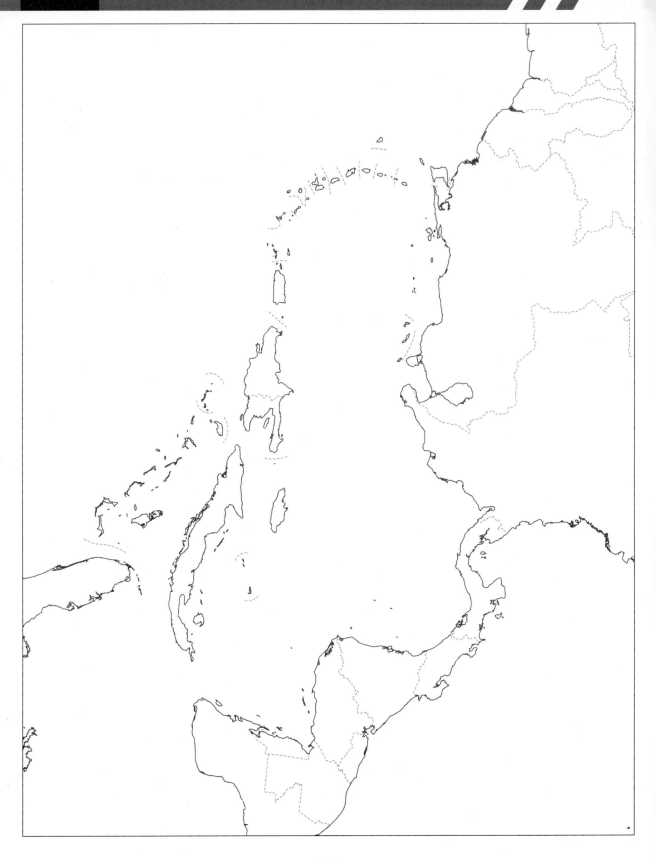

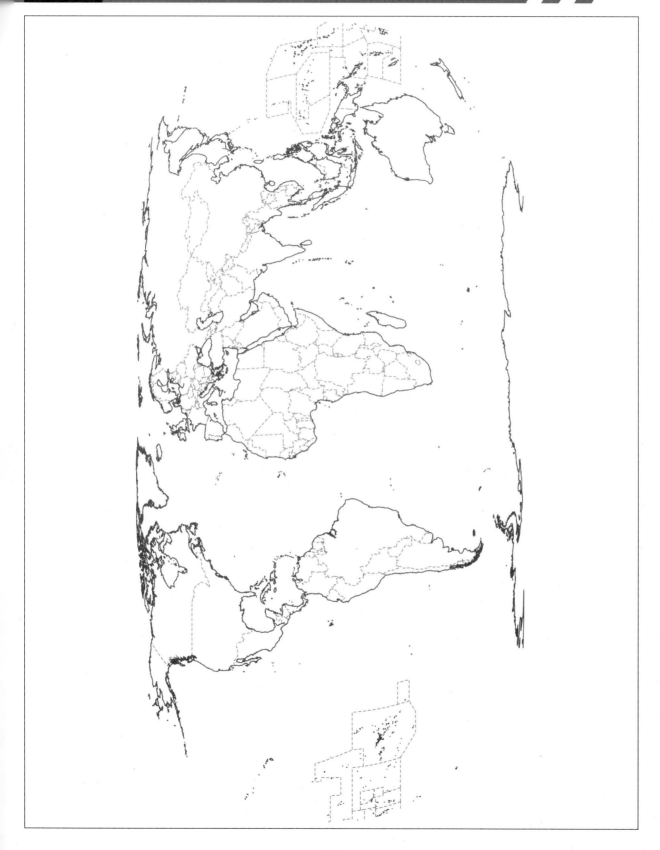

Skills Index

MAIN SKILLS	Workbook Page
Adding information to a map	p26 – Hurricanes
	p44 – Jamaica Features
	p47 – Haiti and the Dominican Republic
	p55 – Antigua
	p60 – Settlements in St Lucia
	p65 – The ABC islands
	p73 – The River Essequibo
	p82 – Africa map
	p90 – Antarctica
	p105 – Mega cities
	p106 – My Caribbean map
	p107 – World Map
	p24 – The Caribbean – physical
	p33 – Caribbean history and heritage
	p34 – African enslavement in the Caribbean
	p39 – The Bahamas
	p41 – People in The Bahamas
	p61 – Island chain
	p76 – Central America in maps
Adding information to a timeline	p48 – Different histories
Annotating a diagram	p100 – Moving plates
	P27 – Caribbean earthquakes
Asian country place knowledge	p86 – Asian countries A-Z
Asian physical features place knowledge	p87 – Asia physical features
Caribbean place knowledge	p22 – The Caribbean – political
	p24 – The Caribbean – physical
Comparing climate types	p96 – Four different climates
Comparing continent by size	p94 – Continents
Comparing different islands	p52 – Caribbean islands word search
Comparing different map types	p6 – Different types of map
Comparing different sources of information	p42 – Cuba – True or false?
Comparing different types of atlas information	p9 – Different types of information
Comparing environmental problems	p103 – Picture tower
Comparing ocean islands	p89 – Coral islands and volcanic islands
Comparing place names	p54 – Place names
Comparing problems	p102 – Serious issues
Compass directions	p22 – The Caribbean – political
Compiling a data set	p67 – Trinidad and Tobago in numbers

Compiling a fact file	p79 – North America physical features
	p87 – Asia physical features
	p98 – World vegetation
	p49 – Puerto Rico
	p50 – US Virgin Islands
	p58 – Exploring Dominica
Compiling data about physical and human geography	p72 – Guyana fact file
Completing a geographical portrait	p50 – US Virgin Islands
Constructing a bar chart	p104 – Cities worldwide
Constructing a bar chart	p67 – Trinidad and Tobago in numbers
Constructing a data list	p41 – People in The Bahamas
Constructing a desire line diagram	p102 – Serious issues
Constructing a map with symbols	p63 – Barbados economic activity
Constructing a model diagram	p103 – Picture tower
Developing place knowledge	p16 – Latitude and longitude
	p19 – Direction finder
	p76 – Central America in maps
	p77 – Central America in words
Devising a route	p32 – Caribbean tourism
Discussing environmental problems	p37 – Threats to the environment
Drawing a bar graph	p31 – Caribbean population and languages
Drawing a cross section diagram	p53 – St Kitts cross section
	p68 – Rain shadow
Drawing a map	p8 – Features map
	p59 – Mount Pelée
Drawing a scale bar	p11 – Large and small scale maps
Drawing a scaled diagram	p95 – Mountains
Drawing a sketch map	p40 – A Cruise in the Bahamas
Drawing maps of islands	p51 – Caribbean island cube
Drawing routes on a map	p32 – Caribbean tourism
Europe place knowledge	p84 – Europe grid squares
Extended learning exercise	p16 – Latitude and longitude
	P27 – Caribbean earthquakes
	p33 – Caribbean history and heritage
	p34 – African enslavement in the Caribbean
	p45 – Jamaica Climate
	p68 – Rain shadow
	p70 – Reviewing the history, tourism and culture of Trinidad
	p72 – Guyana fact file
	p73 – The River Essequibo

Extracting data from a table	p31 – Caribbean population and languages
Extracting information from a bar chart	p45 – Jamaica Climate
Extracting information from a map	P30 – Caribbean energy and minerals
	p39 – The Bahamas
	p42 – Cuba – True or false?
	p43 – Exploring the Cayman Islands
	p49 – Puerto Rico
	p52 – Caribbean islands word search
	p53 – St Kitts cross section
	p54 – Place names
	p79 – North America physical features
	p86 – Asian countries A-Z
	p89 – Coral islands and volcanic islands
	p95 – Mountains
	p104 – Cities worldwide
Extracting information from a map	p66 – Trinidad and Tobago – True or false?
Extracting information from graphs	p46 – Reviewing the history, culture and tourism of Jamaica
Extracting information from maps and charts	p96 – Four different climates
Extracting information from maps, diagrams and text	p56 – Antigua and Barbuda facts
Extracting information from pie charts	p62 – Spice island
Finding out about volcanic eruptions	p59 – Mount Pelée
Identifying barriers	p85 – European journeys
Identifying continents	p90 – World countries
	p94 – Continents
Identifying global time zones	p17 – Time zones
Identifying world cities	p17 – Time zones
Internet research	p90 – Antarctica
Learning about a habitat	p99 – In the tropical forest
Learning about African countries and capitals	p83 – Africa countries game
Learning about Caribbean mineral resources	P30 – Caribbean energy and minerals
Learning about economic activity	p62 – Spice island
Learning about hazards	p101 – Hidden hazards
Learning about seasons	P21 – The Seasons
Learning about the hemispheres	p15 – Different hemispheres
Learning about the Tropics	P21 – The Seasons
Making a bar chart	p57 – Exploring Guadeloupe
Making a model	p28 – Volcano model
Making a plan of a familiar area	p5 – Plan views
Making a rain shadow diagram	p68 – Rain shadow

Making comparisons between places	p43 – Exploring the Cayman Islands
	p57 – Exploring Guadeloupe
Naming and recognising continents	p15 – Different hemispheres
Naming capital towns	p51 – Caribbean island cube
Oceania place knowledge	p88 – Oceania latitude and longitude
Ordering events	p33 – Caribbean history and heritage
Planning a route	p40 – A Cruise in the Bahamas
Planning and drawing a map of a route	p69 – Trinidad mystery tour
Reading a map for information	p77 – Central America in words
Reading for information	p63 – Barbados economic activity
	p34 – African enslavement in the Caribbean
	p37 – Threats to the environment
	p46 – Reviewing the history, culture and tourism of Jamaica
	p48 – Different histories
	p70 – Reviewing the history, tourism and culture of Trinidad
	p99 – In the tropical forest
Recognising climate patterns	p97 – World winds
Recognising country shapes	p80 – South America countries
	p93 – Country card game
Recognising geographical patterns	p81 – South America capital cities
Recognising key words	p64 – All about Barbados
Recognising map symbols	p47 – Haiti and the Dominican Republic
Recognising patterns	p41 – People in The Bahamas
	p45 – Jamaica Climate
Recognising settlement patterns	p60 – Settlements in St Lucia
Researching environmental issues	p38 – Learning about the environment
South America place knowledge	p80 – South America countries
South America place knowledge	p81 – South America capital cities
STEAM activity	p28 – Volcano model
	p51 – Caribbean island cube
	p75 – Finding out about Belize
	p83 – Africa countries game
	p93 – Country card game
	p103 – Picture tower
Tracing a journey along a river	p73 – The River Essequibo
Tracking a route	p26 – Hurricanes
Understanding latitude and longitude	p78 – North American cites
Understanding the structure of volcanoes	p28 – Volcano model
Understanding what causes a volcano	p100 – Moving plates
Understanding what causes earthquakes	P27 – Caribbean earthquakes

Using compass points	p13 – Using a scale bar
Using a scale bar	p61 – Island chain
	p11 – Large and small scale maps
Using a scale bar	p13 – Using a scale bar
	p20 – Directions and distance
	p85 – European journeys
Using an atlas index	p18 – Grid references
Using and making symbols to convey information	p7 – Map symbols
Using compass directions	p19 – Direction finder
	p20 – Directions and distance
	p97 – World winds
Using diamond ranking to compare opinions	p75 – Finding out about Belize
Using different techniques to present information	p10 – School information
Using geographical vocabulary	p98 – World vegetation
	p101 – Hidden hazards
Using grid references	p18 – Grid references
	p44 – Jamaica Features
	p78 – North American cites
	p84 – Europe grid squares
Using latitude and longitude	p16 – Latitude and longitude
	p88 – Oceania latitude and longitude
Using map grid squares	p74 – Guyana grid squares
Using symbols	p55 – Antigua
	p82 – Africa map
	p8 – Features map
World city place knowledge	p105 – Mega cities
World country knowledge	p90 – World countries
World place knowledge	p93 – Country card game
Writing a geographical portrait	p64 – All about Barbados

Atlas Index

ATLAS PAGE	Workbook Page	MAIN SKILLS
2	p5 – Plan views	Making a plan of a familiar area
3	p6 – Different types of map	Comparing different map types
4–5	p7 – Map symbols	Using and making symbols to convey information
5	p8 – Features map	Drawing a map Using symbols and a key
5	p9 – Different types of information	Comparing different types of atlas information
5	p10 – School information	Using different techniques to present information
6	p11 – Large and small scale maps	Drawing a scale bar Measuring distance using a scale bar
4, **6**, 10–11	p13 – Using a scale bar	Using a scale bar Using compass points
7, 74–75	p15 – Different hemispheres	Learning about the hemispheres Naming and recognising continents
7, 72–73	p16 – Latitude and longitude	Using latitude and longitude Developing place knowledge Extended Learning activity
7	p17 – Time zones	Identifying global time zones Identifying world cities
7, 10–13	p18 – Grid references	Using grid references Using an atlas index
7, 60, 64	p19 – Direction finder	Using compass directions Developing place knowledge
7, 10–11, 58–59	p20 – Directions and distance	Using compass directions Using a scale bar
8–9	P21 – The Seasons	Learning about seasons Learning about the Tropics
10–11	p22 – The Caribbean – political	Caribbean place knowledge Compass directions
12–13	p24 – The Caribbean – physical	Caribbean place knowledge Annotating a map
15	p26 – Hurricanes	Adding information to a map Tracking a route

16	P27 – Caribbean earthquakes	Understanding what causes earthquakes
		Annotating a diagram
		Extended Learning activity
17	p28 – Volcano model	Understanding the structure of volcanoes
		Making a model
18	P30 – Caribbean energy and minerals	Extracting information from a map
		Learning about Caribbean mineral resources
19	p31 – Caribbean population and languages	Extracting data from a table
		Drawing a bar graph
19	p32 Caribbean tourism	Drawing routes on a map
		Devising a route
20–21	p33 – Caribbean history and heritage	Annotating a map
		Ordering events
		Extended learning exercise
20–21	p34 – African enslavement in the Caribbean	Reading for information
		Annotating a map
		Extended learning exercise
22–23	p37 – Threats to the environment	Reading for information
		Discussing environmental problems
22–23	p38 – Learning about the environment	Researching environmental issues
24	p39 – The Bahamas	Annotating a map
		Extracting information from a map
24	p40 – A Cruise in the Bahamas	Planning a route
		Drawing a sketch map
24–25	p41 – People in The Bahamas	Constructing a data list
		Annotating a map
		Recognising patterns
26	p42 – Cuba – True or false?	Extracting information from a map
		Comparing different sources of information
27	p43 – Exploring the Cayman Islands	Making comparisons
		Extracting information from a map
28–29	p44 – Jamaica Features	Using grid references
		Adding information to a map

14, **28–32**	p45 – Jamaica Climate	Extracting information from a bar chart Recognising patterns Extended Learning exercise
33	p46 – Reviewing the history, culture and tourism of Jamaica	Reading for information Extracting information from graphs
34	p47 – Haiti and the Dominican Republic	Adding information to a map Recognising map symbols
34	p48 – Different histories	Reading for information Adding information to a timeline
35	p49 – Puerto Rico	Extracting information from a map Making a fact file
35	p50 – US Virgin Islands	Making a fact file Completing a geographical portrait
36	p51 – Caribbean island cube	Drawing maps of islands Naming capital towns STEAM activity
36	p52 – Caribbean islands word search	Extracting information from a map Comparing different islands
37, 17	p53 – St Kitts cross section	Extracting information from a map Drawing a cross section diagram
37	p54 – Place names	Extracting information from a map Comparing place names
38	p55 – Antigua	Adding information to a map Using symbols
38	p56 – Antigua and Barbuda facts	Extracting information from maps, diagrams and text
39	p57 – Exploring Guadeloupe	Making a bar chart Making comparisons between places
40	p58 – Exploring Dominica	Using the map to create a fact file
40	p59 – Mount Pelée	Finding out about volcanic eruptions Map drawing
41	p60 – Settlements in St Lucia	Adding information to a map Recognising settlement patterns
42	p61 – Island chain	Annotating a map Measuring distance using a scale
43	p62 – Spice island	Learning about economic activity Extracting information from pie charts
44–45	p63 – Barbados economic activity	Extracting information from a text Constructing a map with symbols

44–45	p64 – All about Barbados	Recognising key words
		Writing a geographical portrait
46	p65 – The ABC islands	Adding information to a map
47–53	p66 – Trinidad and Tobago – True or false?	Reading maps, charts and tables for information
47–53	p67 – Trinidad and Tobago in numbers	Devising a bar chart
		Compiling a data set
49	p68 – Rain shadow	Drawing a cross section diagram
		Making a rain shadow diagram
		Extended Learning exercise
47–53	p69 – Trinidad mystery tour	Planning and drawing a map of a route
51	p70 – Reviewing the history, tourism and culture of Trinidad	Reading for information
		Extended learning activity
54–55	p72 – Guyana fact file	Compiling data about physical and human geography
		Extended Learning exercise
54–55	p73 – The River Essequibo	Adding information to a map
		Tracing a journey along a river
		Extended Learning exercise
54–55	p74 – Guyana grid squares	Using map grid squares
56	p75 – Finding out about Belize	Using diamond ranking to compare opinions
		STEAM activity
57	p76 – Central America in maps	Annotating a map
		Developing place knowledge
57	p77 – Central America in words	Reading a map for information
		Developing place knowledge
58	p78 – North American cites	Using grid references
		Understanding latitude and longitude
59	p79 – North America physical features	Extracting information from a map
		Compiling a fact file
60	p80 – South America countries	Recognising country shapes
		South America place knowledge
60	p81 – South America capital cities	South America place knowledge
		Recognising geographical patterns
63	p82 – Africa map	Adding information to a map
		Using symbols
62	p83 – Africa countries game	Learning about African countries and capitals
		STEAM activity

64–65	p84 – Europe grid squares	Using grid references Europe place knowledge
64–65	p85 – European journeys	Using a scale bar Identifying barriers
66	p86 – Asian countries A–Z	Extracting information from a map Asian country place knowledge
67	p87 – Asia physical features	Compiling a fact file Asian physical features place knowledge
68	p88 – Oceania latitude and longitude	Using latitude and longitude Oceania place knowledge
68–69	p89 – Coral islands and volcanic islands	Extracting information from a map Comparing ocean islands
70	p90 – Antarctica	Adding information to a map Internet research
72–73	p90 – World countries	World country knowledge Identifying continents
72–73	p93 – Country card game	Recognising country shapes World place knowledge STEAM activity
74–75	p94 – Continents	Identifying continents Comparing continent by size
74–75	p95 – Mountains	Extracting information from a map Drawing a scaled diagram
76	p96 – Four different climates	Extracting information from maps and charts Comparing climate types
76	p97 – World winds	Using compass directions Recognising climate patterns
77	p98 – World vegetation	Compiling a fact file Using geographical vocabulary
77	p99 – In the tropical forest	Reading for information Learning about a habitat
78–79	p100 – Moving plates	Adding labels to a diagram Understanding what causes a volcano
78–79	p101 – Hidden hazards	Using geographical vocabulary Learning about hazards
80–81	p102 – Serious issues	Comparing problems Constructing a desire line diagram

80–81	p103 – Picture tower	Comparing environmental problems
		Constructing a model diagram
		STEAM activity
82–83	p104 – Cities worldwide	Extracting information from a map
		Constructing a bar chart
82–83	p105 – Mega cities	Adding information to a map
		World city place knowledge
All pages	p106 – My Caribbean map	Adding information to a map
All pages	p107 – World Map	Adding information to a map

Notes